THOUGHTS
for the
QUIET HOUR

Compiled by
D.L. MOODY

HARVEST HOUSE PUBLISHERS
Eugene, Oregon 97402

Except where otherwise indicated, all Scripture quotations in this book are taken from the King James Version of the Bible.

Verses marked ERV are taken from the (English) Revised Version of the Bible.

THOUGHTS FOR THE QUIET HOUR

This edition Copyright © 1994 by Harvest House Publishers Eugene, Oregon 97402

(Original edition Copyright © 1900 by Fleming H. Revell Company)

Thoughts for the quiet hour / [edited by] D.L. Moody.
      p.   cm.
   Originally published: Chicago : Revell, c1900.
   ISBN 1-56507-275-8
   1. Devotional calendars.   2. Meditations.   I. Moody,
Dwight Lyman, 1837-1899.
BV4810.T47   1994
242'.2—dc20   94-14573
                                              CIP

Printed in the United States of America.

94 95 96 97 98 99 00 01 — 10 9 8 7 6 5 4 3 2 1

Foreword

One of my favorite pastimes is treasure-hunting. Although I'm not much good with a pick and shovel or a deep-sea diving suit, I usually have no problem staking out my claim in the nearest antiquarian bookshop.

For many of us, great books from ages past have become our genuine treasure. For collectors it is not enough to merely collect old books. Much was published in previous centuries that, like much that is published today, was not worth the paper on which it was printed. So the real task of the book-lover is finding that "needle in a haystack" which retains its universal appeal and intrinsic value unfettered by the changing times.

Thoughts for the Quiet Hour has all the qualities of an enduring spiritual classic: It is uplifting, inspiring, challenging, and concise. Moments after I began reading the brittle, yellowed pages, the power of D.L. Moody's well-chosen selections struck me with all the intensity they must have evoked in readers a century ago.

Whether these thoughts are used for personal quiet time or family devotions, or find their way to the pulpit, they are sure to bless all those who take time to be with God. May the Lord bless you as you endeavor to know Him better.

Dean Andreola
Harvest House Publishers

The Life of
Dwight L. Moody

Dwight L. Moody (1837-1899) became the most effective evangelist of the late nineteenth century. Born on a farm in Northfield, Massachusetts, his father died when he was only five, leaving his mother to raise nine children in abject poverty. It is not difficult to understand why Moody left school at thirteen to find his place in the world. From shoe salesman to successful businessman, he moved quickly up the ladder.

After his salvation experience, Moody began using his influence to reach out to the poor and homeless in urban areas—not forgetting his humble beginnings. When he was financially able, he gave up his business and worked full-time at establishing Sunday schools and supporting the efforts of the YMCA.

After the Civil War he continued his work with the Sunday school, where he met Ira D. Sankey, a talented musical director and hymnwriter. Together they felt the call to combine their talents in full-time evangelism. Moody and Sankey sailed to England. Their crusade ended with great success in London, where meeting attendance totaled more than 2.5 million people.

Upon returning to the United States, Moody continued to conduct powerful evangelistic campaigns in many major cities. His use of practical and humorous stories allowed him to share his love for Christ in a very simple yet compelling way. This resulted in thousands of personal decisions for Christ. His love for the lost also led him to start a training center for ministry. In 1886 he started the

Chicago Evangelization Society, known today as Moody Bible Institute.

Having preached face-to-face to over 100 million people during his forty-year career, Moody became ill and died during his last crusade, in December 1899.

Dwight L. Moody's tireless contribution to God's kingdom, and his ceaseless love for the lost, have become his enduring memorial.

THOUGHTS
for the
QUIET HOUR

To the Reader

One of the brightest signs of the times is that many Christians in our young people's societies and churches are observing a "Quiet Hour" daily. In this age of rush and activity we need some special call to go apart and be alone with God for a part of each day. Any man or woman who does this faithfully and earnestly cannot be more than twenty-four hours away from God.

The selections given in this volume were first published in the monthly issues of the *Record of Christian Work*, and were found very helpful for devotional purposes. They are also a mine of thoughts, to light up the verses quoted. Being of permanent value, it has been thought desirable to transfer them from the pages of the magazine to this permanent volume.

May they have a helpful ministry, leading many into closer communion with God!

D. L. Moody

January

January 1

Come up in the morning...and present thyself...to me in the top of the mount.
Exodus 34:2

My Father, I am coming. Nothing on the mean plain shall keep me away from the holy heights. Help me to climb fast, and keep Thou my foot, lest it fall upon the hard rock! At Thy bidding I come, so Thou wilt not mock my heart. Bring with Thee honey from heaven, yea, milk and wine, and oil for my soul's good, and stay the sun in his course, or the time will be too short in which to look upon Thy face and to hear Thy gentle voice.

Morning on the mount! It will make me strong and glad all the rest of the day so well begun.   *Joseph Parker*

January 2

My reward is with me.   Revelation 22:12

We are to be rewarded, not only for work done, but for burdens borne, and I am not sure but that the brightest rewards will be for those who have borne burdens without murmuring. On that day He will take the lily, that has been growing so long among thorns, and lift it up to be the glory and wonder of all the universe; and the fragrance of that lily will draw forth ineffable praises from all the hosts of heaven.
Andrew Bonar

January 3

Where art thou? Genesis 3:9

Art thou hiding thyself away from Him who would send thee forth to do His own blessed work in His own way? Oh, let me say to thee, "The Lord hath need of thee." It may seem to be only a little thing He has for thee to do, but it is an important one. He has "need of thee." Turn not thy back upon Him; put not thyself out of the way of being employed by Him; do not begin by laying down laws for thyself as to what thou wilt do and what thou wilt not do; but cry out from the very depth of thy heart, "Here am I, send me." *W. Hay Aitken*

January 4

Many are the afflictions of the righteous, but the Lord delivereth him out of them all.
Psalm 34:19

All the afflictions of the righteous open out into something glorious. The prisoner is not merely delivered, but he finds an angel waiting for him at the door. And with every deliverance comes a specific blessing. One angel is named faith; another, love; another, joy; another, long suffering; another, gentleness; another, goodness; another, meekness; another, temperance; another, peace. Each of these graces says, "We have come out of great tribulation." *G. Bowen*

January 5

The Lord is my . . . song. Psalm 118:14

Let us think of God Himself becoming our song. This is the fullness and perfection of knowing God: so to know Him that He Himself becomes our delight; so to know Him that praise is sweetest, and fullest, and freshest, and gladdest, when we sing of Him. He who has learned this blessed secret carries the golden key of heaven—nay, he hath fetched heaven down to earth, and need not envy the angels now.   *Mark Guy Pearse*

January 6

Fear ye not, stand still, and see the salvation of the Lord.   Exodus 14:13

Often God seems to place His children in positions of profound difficulty—leading them into a wedge from which there is no escape; contriving a situation no human judgment would have permitted, had it been previously consulted. The very cloud conducts them thither. You may be thus involved at this very hour. It does seem perplexing and very serious to the last degree; but it is perfectly right. The issue will more than justify Him who has brought you hither. It is a platform for the display of His almighty grace and power. He will not only deliver you, but in doing so He will give you a lesson that you will never forget and to which, in many a psalm and song in after days, you will revert. You will never be able to thank God enough for having done just as He has.   *F. B. Meyer*

January 7

Now are ye light in the Lord; walk as children of light.   Ephesians 5:8

The influence we exert in the world is created

by our relationship to Jesus Christ and our relationship to Jesus Christ is revealed by our influence.   *Selected*

January 8

Take good heed therefore unto yourselves.
Joshua 23:11

Gold cannot be used for currency as long as it is mixed with quartz and rock in which it lies embedded. So your soul is useless to God till taken out from sin and earthliness and selfishness, in which it lies buried. By the regenerating power of the Spirit you must be separated unto Christ, stamped with His image and superscription, and made into a divine currency, which shall bear His likeness among men. The Christian is, so to speak, the circulating medium of Christ, the coin of the realm by whom the great transactions of mercy and grace to a lost world are carried on. As the currency stands for the gold, so does the Christian stand for Christ, representing His good and acceptable will.
A. J. Gordon

January 9

He that is faithful in that which is least is faithful also in much.   Luke 16:10

The least action of life can be as surely done from the loftiest motive as the highest and noblest. Faithfulness measures acts as God measures them. True conscientiousness deals with our duties as God deals with them. Duty is duty, conscience is conscience, right is right,

and wrong is wrong, whatever sized type they be printed in. "Large" and "small" are not words for the vocabulary of conscience. It knows only two words—right and wrong.
Alexander Maclaren

January 10

My God shall supply all your need according to His riches in glory by Christ Jesus.
Philippians 4:19

What a source—"God"! What a standard—"His riches in glory"! What a channel—"Christ Jesus"! It is your sweet privilege to place *all your need* over against *His riches,* and lose sight of the former in the presence of the latter. His exhaustless treasury is thrown open to you, in all the love of His heart; go and draw upon it, in the artless simplicity of faith, and you will never have occasion to look to a creature-stream, or lean on a creature-prop.   *C. H. Mackintosh*

January 11

Count it all joy when ye fall into diverse temptations.   James 1:2

We cannot be losers by trusting God, for He is honored by faith, and most honored when faith discerns His love and truth behind a thick cloud of His ways and providence. Happy those who are thus tried! Let us only be clear of unbelief and a guilty conscience. We shall hide ourselves in the rock and pavilion of the Lord, sheltered beneath the wings of everlasting love till all calamities be overpast.   *Selected*

January 12

*Blessed are they that have not seen
and yet have believed.*   John 20:29

The seen are shadows: the substance is found
in the unseen . . . . No doubt, in Christ, the foundation of our faith is unseen; but so is that of
yonder tower that lifts its tall erect form among
the waves over which it throws a saving light. It
appears to rest on the rolling billows; but
beneath these, invisible and immovable, lies the
solid rock on which it stands secure; and when
the hurricane roars above, and breakers roar
below, I could go calmly to sleep in that lone seat
tower. Founded on a rock, and safer than the
proudest palace that stands on the sandy, surf-
beaten shore, it cannot be moved. Still less the
Rock of Ages! Who trusts in that is fit for death,
prepared for judgment, ready for the last day's
sounding trumpet, since "the Lord redeemeth
the soul of His servants, and none of them that
trust in Him shall be desolate."   *Guthrie*

January 13

*Herein is my Father glorified, that ye bear
much fruit.*   John 15:8

What a possibility, what an inspiration, that
we can enhance the glory of "our Father"! Our
hearts leap at the thought.

How can this be done? By bearing "leaves"—
a *profession* of love for Him? No. By bearing
some fruit? No. "That ye bear *much* fruit." In the

abundance of the yield is the joy, the glory of the husbandman. We should therefore aim to be extraordinary, "hundredfold" Christians, satisfied with none but the largest yield. Our lives should be packed with good deeds. Then at harvesttime we can say, "Father, I have glorified Thee on the earth!"   *W. Jennings*

January 14

Every day will I bless Thee, and I will
praise Thy name for ever and ever.
Psalm 145:2

There is a very beautiful device by which the Japanese are accustomed to express their wishes for their friends. It is the figure of a drum in which the birds have built their nest. The story told of it is that once there lived a good king, so anxiously concerned for the welfare of his people that at the palace gate he set a drum, and whoever had any wrong to be redressed or any want should beat the drum, and at once, by day or night, the king would grant the suppliant an audience and relief. But throughout the land there reigned such prosperity and contentment that none needed to appeal for anything, and the birds built their nests within it and filled it with the music of their song.

Such gracious access is granted to us even by the King of heaven, and day and night His ready hearing and His help are within the reach of all that come to Him; but of all men most blessed are they who have found on earth a blessedness in which all want is forgotten, and trust rests so assured of safety in the Father's care that prayer gives place to ceaseless praise. They *rejoice in the Lord always.*   *Mark Guy Pearse*

January 15

They shall mount up with wings as eagles; they shall run and not be weary; they shall walk and not faint.   Isaiah 40:31

This, my soul, is the triumph of thy being— to be able to *walk* with God! Flight belongs to the young soul; it is the *romance* of religion. To run without weariness belongs to the *lofty* soul; it is the *beauty* of religion. But to walk and not faint belongs to the *perfect* soul; it is the *power* of religion.

Canst thou walk in white through the stained thoroughfares of men? Canst thou touch the vile and polluted ones of earth and retain thy garments pure? Canst thou meet in contact with the sinful and be thyself undefiled? *Then* thou hast surpassed the flight of the eagle!
George Matheson

January 16

Moses was in the mount forty days and forty nights.   Exodus 24:18

The life of fellowship with God cannot be built up in a day. It begins with the habitual reference of all to Him, hour by hour, as Moses did in Egypt. But it moves on to more and longer periods of communion; and it finds its consummation and bliss in days and nights of intercession and waiting and holy intercourse.
F. B. Meyer

January 17

Elisha said, "Lord, I pray Thee, open his eyes that he may see." 2 Kings 6:17

This is the prayer we need to pray for ourselves and for one another: "Lord, open our eyes that we may see"; for the world all around us, as well as around the prophet, is full of God's horses and chariots, waiting to carry us to places of glorious victory. And when our eyes are thus opened, we shall see in all the events of life, whether great or small, whether joyful or sad, a "chariot" for our souls. Everything that comes to us becomes a chariot the moment we treat it as such; on the other hand, even the smallest trial may be a juggernaut to crush us into misery or despair if we so consider it. It lies with each of us to choose which they shall be. It all depends, not upon what these events are, but upon how we take them. If we lie down under them, and let them roll over us and crush us, they become juggernauts, but if we climb up into them, as into a car of victory, and make them carry us triumphantly onward and upward, they become the chariots of God. *Smith*

January 18

All things work together for good to them that love God. Romans 8:28

In one thousand trials it is not five hundred of them that work for the believer's good, but nine hundred and ninety-nine of them, AND ONE BESIDE. *George Mueller*

January 19

Thou shalt make holy garments for Aaron.
Exodus 28:2

Have we no garments of blue, and purple, and beautiful suggestiveness? We have garments of praise; we are clothed with the Lord Jesus. And have we no ornaments? The ornament of a meek and quiet spirit is, in the sight of God, of great price. And have we no golden bells? We have the golden bells of holy actions. Our words are bells, our actions are bells, our purposes are bells. Wherever we move, our motion is thus understood to be a motion toward holy places, holy deeds, holy character.
Joseph Parker

January 20

My voice shalt Thou hear in the morning,
O Lord; in the morning will I direct
my prayer unto Thee, and will look up.
Psalm 5:3

The morning is the gate of the day, and should be well guarded with prayer. It is one end of the thread on which the day's actions are strung, and should be well knotted with devotion. If we felt more the majesty of life we should be more careful of its mornings. He who rushes from his bed to his business and waiteth not to worship is as foolish as though he had not put on his clothes, or cleansed his face, and as unwise as through he dashed into battle without arms or armor. Be it ours to bathe in the softly flowing river of communion with God, before the heat of the wilderness and the burden of the way begin to oppress us.   *Spurgeon*

January 21

Show me Thy ways, O Lord; teach me Thy paths.   Psalm 25:4

There is a path in which every child of God is to walk, and in which alone God can accompany him.   *Denham Smith*

January 22

There remaineth therefore a rest to the people of God.   Hebrews 4:9

How sweet the music of this first heavenly chime floating across the waters of death from the towers of the New Jerusalem. Pilgrim, faint under thy long and arduous pilgrimage, hear it! It is REST. Soldier, carrying still upon thee blood and dust of battle, hear it! It is REST. Voyager, tossed on the waves of sin and sorrow, driven hither and tither on the world's heaving ocean of vicissitude, hear it! The haven is in sight; the very waves that are breaking on thee seem to murmur, *"So He giveth His beloved REST."* It is the long-drawn sigh of existence at last answered. The toil and travail of earth's protracted week is at an end. The calm of its unbroken Sabbath is begun. Man, weary man, has found at last the long-sought-for *rest* in the bosom of his God!
Macduff

January 23

Under His shadow.   Song of Solomon 2:3

I seem to see four pictures suggested by that phrase: Under the shadow of a rock in a weary plain; under the shadow of a tree; closer still, under the shadow of His wing; nearest and closest, in the shadow of His hand. Surely that hand must be the pierced hand, that may oftentimes press us sorely, and yet evermore encircling, upholding, and shadowing!
Frances Ridley Havergal

January 24

He made as though He would have gone further.   Luke 24:28

Is not God always acting thus? He comes to *us* by His Holy Spirit as He did to these two disciples. He speaks to us through the preaching of the gospel, through the Word of God, through the various means of grace and the providential circumstances of life; and having thus spoken, He makes as though He would go further. If the ear be opened to His voice and the heart to His Spirit, the prayer will then go up, "Lord, abide with me." But if that voice makes no impression, then He passes on, as He has done thousands of times, leaving the heart at each time harder than before, and the ear more closed to the Spirit's call.   *F. Whitfield*

January 25

My God shall be my strength.   Isaiah 49:5

Oh, do not pray for easy lives! Pray to be stronger men! Do not pray for tasks equal to your powers; pray for powers equal to your tasks! Then the doing of your work shall be no miracle, but *you* shall be a miracle. Every day you shall wonder at yourself, at the richness of life which has come in you by the grace of God. *Phillips Brooks*

January 26

Despising the shame.   Hebrews 12:2

And how is that to be done? In two ways. Go up the mountain, and the things in the plain will look very small; the higher you rise the more insignificant they will seem. Hold fellowship with God, and the threatening foes here will seem very, very unformidable. Another way is to pull up the curtain and gaze on what is behind it. The low foothills that lie at the base of some Alpine country may look high when seen from the plain, as long as the snowy summits are wrapped in mist; but when a little puff of wind comes and clears away the fog from the lofty peaks, nobody looks at the little green hills in front. So the world's hindrances and the world's difficulties and cares look very lofty till the cloud lifts. But when we see the great white summits, everything lower does not seem so very high after all. Look to Jesus, and that will dwarf the difficulties.   *Alexander Maclaren*

January 27

Are there not twelve hours in the day?
John 11:9

The very fact of a Christian being here, and not in heaven, is a proof that some work awaits him.   *William Arnot*

January 28

Not as I will, but as Thou wilt.
Matthew 26:39

There are no disappointments to those whose wills are buried in the will of God.   *Faber*

January 29

The living God.   Daniel 6:20

How many times we find this expression in the Scriptures, and yet it is just this very thing that we are so prone to lose sight of! We know it is written *"the living God,"* but in our daily life there is scarcely anything we practically so much lose sight of as the fact that God is THE LIVING GOD; that He is now whatever He was three or four thousand years since; that He has the same sovereign power, the same saving love toward those who love and serve Him as ever He had, and that He will do for them now what He did for others two, three, four thousand years ago, simply because He is the living God, the unchanging One. Oh, how therefore we should confide in Him, and in our darkest moments never lose sight of the fact that He *is* still and ever *will be* THE LIVING GOD!   *George Mueller*

January 30

Therefore we are buried with Him by baptism into death that like as Christ was raised up from the dead by the glory of the Father, even so we also should walk in newness of life.
Romans 6:4

That is the life we are called upon to live, and that is the life it is our privilege to lead; for God never gives us a call without its being a privilege, and He never gives us the privilege to come up higher without stretching out to us His hand to lift us up. Come up higher and higher into the realities and glories of the resurrection life, knowing that your life is hid with Christ in God. Shake yourself loose of every encumbrance, turn your back on every defilement, give yourself over like clay to the hands of the potter, that He may stamp upon you the fullness of His own resurrection glory, that you, beholding as in a mirror the glory of the Lord, may be changed from glory to glory as by the Spirit of the Lord.   *W. Hay Aitken*

January 31

Christ is all and in all.   Colossians 3:11

> The *service* of Christ is the *business* of my life.
> The *will* of Christ is the *law* of my life.
> The *presence* of Christ is the *joy* of my life.
> The *glory* of Christ is the *crown* of my life.

Selected

February

February 1

Continue in prayer.   Colossians 4:2

Dost thou want nothing? Then I fear thou dost not know thy poverty. Hast thou no mercy to ask of God? Then may the Lord's mercy show thee thy misery. A prayerless soul is a Christless soul. Prayer is the lisping of the believing infant, the shout of the fighting believer, the requiem of the dying saint falling asleep in Jesus.   *Spurgeon*

February 2

In whom all the building, fitly framed together, groweth unto an holy temple in the Lord.
Ephesians 2:21

The life-tabernacle is a wondrous building; there is room for workers of all kinds in the uprearing of its mysterious and glorious walls. If we cannot do the greatest work, we may do the least. Our heaven will come out of the realization of the fact that it was God's tabernacle we were building, and under God's blessing that we were working.   *Joseph Parker*

February 3

Love not the world.   1 John 2:15

Love it not, and yet love it. Love it with the love of Him who gave His Son to die for it. Love it with the love of Him who shed His blood for it. Love it with the love of angels, who rejoice in its conversion. Love it to do it good, giving your tears to its sufferings, your pity to its sorrows, your wealth to its wants, and your prayers to its miseries. To its fields of charity, and philanthropy, and Christian piety, give your powers and hours of labor. You cannot live without affecting the world or being affected by it. You will make it better, or it will make you worse.

God help you by His grace and Holy Spirit so to live in the world as to live above it and look beyond it, and so to love it that when you leave it you may leave it better than you found it.
Guthrie

February 4

Thou openest Thine hand and satisfiest the desire of every living thing. Psalm 145:16

Desire—it is a dainty word! It were much that He should satisfy the *need,* the *want;* but He goeth far beyond that. Pity is moved to meet our need; duty may sometimes look after our wants; but to satisfy the *desire* implies a tender watchfulness, a sweet and gracious knowledge of us, an eagerness of blessing. God is never satisfied until He has satisfied our desires.
Mark Guy Pearse

February 5

Ye servants of the Lord, which by night stand in the house of the Lord ....The Lord that made heaven and earth bless thee out of Zion. Psalm 134:1,3

If I would know the love of my friend, I must see what it can do in the winter. So with the divine love. It is very easy for me to worship in the summer sunshine, when the melodies of life are in the air and the fruits of life are on the tree. But let the song of the bird cease, and the fruit of the tree fall; and will my heart still go on to sing? Will I stand in God's house by night? Will I love Him in His own night? Will I watch with Him even one hour in His Gethsemane? Will I help to bear His cross up the Via Dolorosa? My love has come to Him in His humiliation. My faith has found Him in His lowliness. My heart has recognized His majesty through His mean disguise, and I know at last that I desire not the gift, but the Giver. When I can stand in His house by night, I have accepted Him for Himself alone.   *George Matheson*

February 6

He that saith he abideth in Him ought himself also so to walk even as He walked.
1 John 2:6

The preaching that this world needs most is the *sermons in shoes* that are walking with Jesus Christ.   *Selected*

February 7

Then shall we know, if we follow on to know the Lord.   Hosea 6:3

The Lord has brought us into the pathway of the knowledge of Him, and bids us pursue that path through all its strange meanderings until it opens out upon the plain where God's throne is. Our life is a following on to know the Lord.

We marvel at some of the experiences through which we are called to pass, but afterward we see that they afforded us some new knowledge of our Lord.... We have not to wait for some brighter opportunity, but by improvement of the present are to build for ourselves a bridge to that future. *G. Bowen*

February 8

Get thee out of thy country, and from thy kindred, and from thy father's house.
Genesis 12:1

Abraham ... was gathered to his people.
Genesis 25:8

After all communion we dwell as upon islands, dotted over a great archipelago, each upon his little rock with the sea dashing between us; but the time comes when, if our hearts are set upon that great Lord whose presence makes us one, there shall be no more sea and all the isolated rocks shall be parts of a great continent....If we cultivate that sense of detachment from the present and of having our true affinities in the unseen, if we dwell here as strangers because our citizenship is in heaven, then death will not drag us away from our associates nor hunt us into a lonely land, but will bring us where closer bonds shall knit the "sweet societies" together, and the sheep shall couch close by one another because all gather round the one Shepherd. Then many a tie shall be re-woven, and the solitary wanderer shall meet again the dear ones whom he had "loved long since and lost awhile."
Alexander Maclaren

February 9

Therefore will the Lord wait, that He may be gracious unto you.   Isaiah 30:18

This is God's way. In the darkest hours of the night His tread draws near across the billows. As the day of execution is breaking, the angel comes to Peter's cell. When the scaffold for Mordecai is complete, the royal sleeplessness leads to a reaction in favor of the threatened race.

Ah, soul, it may have come to the worst with thee ere thou art delivered; but thou wilt be! God may keep thee waiting, but He will ever be mindful of His covenant, and will appear to fulfill His inviolable Word.   *F. B. Meyer*

February 10

He loveth our nation and he hath built us a synagogue.   Luke 7:5

Marble and granite are perishable monuments, and their inscriptions may be seldom read. *Carve your names on human hearts;* they alone are immortal!   *Theodore Cuyler*

February 11

As many as I love I . . . chasten.   Revelation 3:19

I once saw a dark shadow resting on the bare side of a hill. Seeking its cause, I saw a little cloud, bright as the light, floating in the clear blue above. Thus it is with our sorrow. It may be dark and cheerless here on earth, yet look above and you shall see it to be but a shadow of His brightness whose name is Love.   *Dean Alford*

February 12

What mean these stones?   Joshua 4:21.

Ye also as living stones.   1 Peter 2:5 ERV

There should be something so remarkable, so peculiar, about the life and conversation of a Christian that men should be compelled to ask, "What does this mean?" ... Is there anything in your character, words, and habits of life so different from the world around you that men are involuntarily compelled to ask themselves or others, "What does this mean?" Not that there is to be a forced singularity, a peculiarity for the sake of being peculiar; that were merely to copy the Pharisaism of ancient days....Oh, that we might realize that this is the purpose for which God sends us into the world, as He sent His only begotten Son!   *S.A. Blackwood*

February 13

All ... saw his face as it had been the face of an angel.   Acts 6:15

The face is made every day by its morning prayer, and by its morning look out of windows which open upon heaven.   *Joseph Parker*

February 14

At the commandment of the Lord they rested in the tents, and at the commandment of the Lord they journeyed.   Numbers 9:23

This is the secret of peace and calm elevation. If an Israelite in the desert had taken it into his head to make some movement indepen-dent of Jehovah, if he took it upon him to move when the crowd was at rest, or to halt while the crowd was moving, we can easily see what the result would have been. And so it will ever be with us. If we move when we ought to rest, or rest when we ought to move, we shall not have the divine presence with us.   *C. H. Mackintosh*

February 15

In whom also, after that ye believed, ye were sealed with that Holy Spirit of promise.
Ephesians 1:13

The Lord puts a seal upon His own, that everybody may know them. The sealing in your case is the Spirit producing in you likeness to the Lord. The holier you become, the seal is more distinct and plain, the more evident to every passerby, for then will men take knowl-edge of you that you have been with Jesus.
Andrew Bonar

February 16

Boast not thyself of tomorrow.   Proverbs 27:1

The only preparation for the morrow is the right use of today. The stone in the hands of the builder must be put in its place and fitted to receive another. The morrow comes for naught if today is not heeded. Neglect not the call that comes to thee this day, for such neglect is noth-ing else than boasting thyself of tomorrow.
G. Bowen

February 17

"I will help thee," saith the Lord.   Isaiah 12:14

O my soul, is not this enough? Dost thou need more strength than the omnipotence of the united Trinity? Dost thou want more wisdom than exists in the Father, more love than displays itself in the Son, or more power than is manifest in the influences of the Spirit? Bring hither thine empty pitcher! Surely this well will fill it. Haste, gather up thy wants, and bring them here—thine emptiness, thy woes, thy needs. Behold, this river of God is full for thy supply; what canst thou desire beside? Go forth, my soul, in this thy might. The eternal God is thine helper!   *Spurgeon*

February 18

To every man his work.   Mark 13:34

He does the most for God's great world who does the best in his own little world.   *Selected*

February 19

Bring of the fish which ye have now caught. John 21:10

Why was this? Oh, the Lord wants us to minister to Him as well as to receive from Him, and our service finds its true end when it becomes food for our dear Lord. He was pleased to feed on their fish while they were feeding on His. It was the double banquet of which He speaks in the tender message of revelation, "I will sup with him, and he with me."   *A. B. Simpson*

February 20

By faith Abraham, when he was called to go out into a place which he should after receive for an inheritance, obeyed. Hebrews 11:8

Whither he went, he knew not; it was enough for him to know that he went with God. He leaned not so much upon the promises as upon the Promiser. He looked not on the difficulties of his lot but on the King—eternal, immortal, invisible, the only wise God, who had deigned to appoint his course and would certainly vindicate Himself. O glorious faith! This is thy work, these are thy possibilities: contentment to sail with sealed orders because of unwavering confidence in the love and wisdom of the Lord High Admiral; willingness to rise up, leave all, and follow Christ because of the glad assurance that earth's best cannot bear comparison with Heaven's least. *F. B. Meyer*

February 21

The Lord is a God of knowledge, and by Him actions are weighed. 1 Samuel 2:3

God does not *measure* what we bring to Him. He *weighs* it. *Mark Guy Pearse*

February 22

After ye were illuminated ye endured a great fight of afflictions. Hebrews 10:32

Our boldness for God *before the world* must always be the result of individual dealing with

God *in secret.* Our victories over self and sin and the world are always first fought where no eye sees but God's....If we have not these *secret* conflicts, well may we not have any *open* ones. The *outward* absence of conflict betrays the *inward* sleep of the soul.   *F. Whitfield*

February 23

Philip findeth Nathaniel and saith unto him, "We have found Him of whom Moses in the law and the prophets did write....Come and see."   John 1:45,46

The next thing to knowing that "we have found Him" is to find someone else, and say, "Come and see."   *Frances Ridley Havergal*

February 24

The wind bloweth where it listeth, and thou hearest the sound thereof but canst not tell whence it cometh and whither it goeth; so is every one that is born of the Spirit.   John 3:8

We know that the wind listeth to blow where there is a vacuum. If you find a tremendous rush of wind, you know that somewhere there is an empty space. I am perfectly sure about this fact: If we could expel all pride, vanity, self-righteousness, self-seeking, desire for applause, honor, and promotion—if by some divine power we should be utterly emptied of all that, the Spirit would come as a rushing mighty wind to fill us.   *A. J. Gordon*

February 25

Thy gentleness hath made me great.
2 Samuel 22:36

The gentleness of Christ is the comeliest ornament that a Christian can wear.
William Arnot

February 26

Jacob went on his way, and the angels of God met him.   Genesis 32:1

It is in the path where God has bade us walk that we shall find the angels around us. We may meet them, indeed, on paths of our own choosing, but it will be the sort of angel that Balaam met, with a sword in his hand, mighty and beautiful, but wrathful too; and we had better not affront him! But the friendly helpers, the emissaries of God's love, the apostles of His grace, do not haunt the roads that we make for ourselves.   *Alexander Maclaren*

February 27

*I am the way, the truth, and the life;
no man cometh unto the Father but by me.*
John 14:6

Heaven often seems distant and unknown, but if He who made the road thither is our guide, we need not fear to lose the way. We do not want to see far ahead—only far enough to discern Him and trace His footsteps....They who follow Christ, even through darkness, will surely reach the Father.   *Henry Van Dyke*

February 28

Forgetting those things which are behind . . .
I press toward the mark for the prize of the
high calling of God in Christ Jesus.
Philippians 3:13,14

It is not by regretting what is irreparable that true work is to be done, but by making the best of what we are. It is not by complaining that we have not the right tools, but by using well the tools we have. What we are, and where we are, is God's providential arrangement—God's doing, though it may be man's misdoing. Life is a series of mistakes, and he is not the best Christian who makes the fewest false steps. He is the best who wins the most splendid victories by the retrieval of mistakes. *F. W. Robertson*

March

March 1

*Come up in the morning . . . and present
thyself unto me in the top of the mount.*
Exodus 34:2

The *morning* is the time fixed for my meeting
the Lord. This very word *morning* is as a cluster
of rich grapes. Let me crush them, and drink
the sacred wine.

In the morning! Then God means me to be
at my best in strength and hope. I have not to
climb in my weakness. In the night I have
buried yesterday's fatigue, and in the morning I
take a new lease of energy.

Sweet morning! There is hope in its music.
Blessed is the day whose morning is sanctified!
Successful is the day whose first victory was won
in prayer! Holy is the day whose dawn finds thee
on the top of the mount! Health is established in
the morning. Wealth is won in the morning.
The light is brightest in the morning. "Wake,
psaltery and harp; I myself will awake early."
Joseph Parker

March 2

*Whatsoever a man soweth, that shall he
also reap.* Galatians 6:7

The most common actions of life, its every
day and hour, are invested with the highest
grandeur when we think how they extend their
issues into eternity. Our hands are now sowing
seeds for that great harvest. We shall meet

again all we are doing and have done. The graves shall give up their dead, and from the tombs of oblivion the past shall give up all that it holds in keeping, to bear true witness for or against us.   *Guthrie*

March 3

There are eleven days' journey from Horeb, by the way of Mount Seir, unto Kadesh-barnea. Deuteronomy 1:2

Eleven days, and yet it took them forty years! How was this? Alas! we need not travel far for the answer. It is only too like ourselves. How slowly we get over the ground! What windings and turnings! How often we have to go back and travel over the same ground again and again. We are slow travelers because we are slow learners. Our God is a faithful and wise, as well as a gracious and patient, Teacher. He will not permit us to pass cursorily over our lessons. Sometimes we think we have mastered a lesson and we attempt to move on to another, but our wise Teacher knows better, and He sees the need of deeper plowing. He will not have us mere theorists or smatterers; He will keep us, if need be, year after year at our scales until we learn to sing.   *C. H. Mackintosh*

March 4

If we confess our sins, He is faithful and just to forgive us our sins, and to cleanse us from all unrighteousness.   1 John 1:9

The same moment which brings the consciousness of sin ought to bring also the confession

of it and the consciousness of forgiveness.
Smith

March 5

*As captain of the host of the Lord am I
now come.*   Joshua 5:14

Surely Israel might now face the foe with
unwavering confidence, and sing of victory
even before the battle was gained. And so may
the Christian. It is to no conflict of uncertain
issue that he advances; the result of the battle is
not doubtful. The struggle may be severe and
the warfare long; he may sometimes, like the
pilgrim, be beaten to the ground and well-nigh
lose his sword; but "though cast down" he is
"not destroyed." The Captain of salvation is on
his side, and in the midst of sharpest conflict he
can say, "Thanks be unto God, who giveth us
the victory through our Lord Jesus Christ."
S. A. Blackwood

March 6

To me to live is Christ, and to die is gain.
Philippians 1:21

Live in Christ, and you are in the suburbs of
heaven. There is but a thin wall between you
and the land of praises. You are within one
hour's sailing of the shore of the new Canaan.
William Rutherford

March 7

*He that sent me is with me; the Father hath
not left me alone, for I do always those things
that please Him.*   John 8:29

He who holds nearest communion with heaven can best discharge the duties of every-day life.   *Selected*

March 8

Quench not the Spirit.   1 Thessalonians 5:19

In order that you may not quench the Spirit, you must make it a constant study to know what is the mind of the Spirit. You must discriminate with the utmost care between His suggestions and the suggestions of your own deceitful heart. You will keep in constant recollection what are the offices of the Spirit as described by Christ in the Gospel of John. You will be on your guard against impulsive movements, inconsiderate acts, rash words. You will abide in prayer. Search the Word. Confess Christ on all possible occasions. Seek the society of His people. Shrink from conformity to the world, its vain fashions, unmeaning etiquette. Be scrupulous in your reading. "What I say unto you I say unto all: Watch!" "Have oil in your lamps." "Quench not the Spirit."   *Bowen*

March 9

When He cometh into the world, He saith...
"A body hast Thou prepared me."   Hebrews 10:5

This word of Christ must be adopted by each of His followers. Nothing will help us to live in this world and keep ourselves unspotted but the Spirit that was in Christ, that looked upon His body as prepared by God for His service; that looks upon our body as prepared by Him too, that we might offer it to Him. Like Christ, we too have a body in which the Holy Spirit dwells. Like Christ, we too must yield our body, with every member, every power, every action, to fulfill His will, to be offered up to Him, to glorify Him. Like Christ, we must prove in our body that we are holy to the Lord.

Andrew Murray

March 10

Full of [satisfied with] years. Genesis 25:8

Scaffoldings are for buildings, and the moments and days and years of our earthly lives are scaffolding. What are you building inside it? What kind of a structure will be disclosed when the scaffolding is knocked away? Days and years are ours, that they may give us what eternity cannot take away—a character built upon the love of God in Christ, and molded into His likeness.

Has your life helped you to do that? If so, you have gotten the best out of it, and your life is completed, whatever may be the number of its days. Quality, not quantity, is the thing that determines the perfectness of a life. Has your life this completeness? *Alexander Maclaren*

March 11

Keep yourselves in the love of God. Jude 21

Fruit ripened in the sun is sweetest. *Selected*

March 12

Ye shall receive power after that the Holy Ghost is come upon you, and ye shall be witnesses unto me.   Acts 1:8

Look at it! Think of it! A hundred and twenty men and women having no patronage, no promise of any earthly favor, no endowment, no wealth—a company of men and women having to get their living by common daily toil, and busied with all the household duties of daily life—and yet *they* are to begin the conquests of Christianity! To them is entrusted a work which is to turn the world upside down. None so exalted but the influence of this lowly company shall reach to them until the throne of the Caesars is claimed for Christ. None so far off but the power of this little band gathered in an upper room shall extend to them until the whole world is knit into a brotherhood! Not a force is there on the earth, either of men or devils, but they shall overcome it, until every knee shall bow to their Master and every tongue shall confess that He is Lord.

A thing impossible, absurd, look at it as you will, until you admit this: *They are to be filled with the Holy Ghost.* Then difficulties melt into the empty air. Then there is no limit to their hopes, for there is no limit to their power. Their strength is not only "as the strength of ten," but it is as the strength of the Almighty.

This is Christ's idea of Christianity; the idea not of man—it is infinitely too sublime—but the idea of God!   *Mark Guy Pearse*

March 13

He that abideth in me, and I in him, the same bringeth forth much fruit; for without me ye can do nothing. John 15:5

Too much taken up with our work, we may forget our Master; it is possible to have the hand full and the heart empty. Taken up with our Master we cannot forget our work; if the heart is filled with His love, how can the hands not be active in His service? *Adolphe Monod*

March 14

He that eateth me, even he shall live by me. John 6:57

To feed on Christ is to get His strength into us to be our strength. You feed on the cornfield, and the strength of the cornfield comes into you and is your strength. You feed on Christ, and then go and live your life; and it is Christ in you that lives your life, that helps the poor, that tells the truth, that fights the battles, and that wins the crown. *Phillips Brooks*

March 15

I sought Him, but I found Him not. Song of Solomon 3:1

Tell me where you lost the company of Christ, and I will tell you the most likely place to find Him. Have you lost Christ in the closet by restraining prayer? Then it is there you must seek and find Him. Did you lose Christ by sin? You will find Him in no other way than by the giving up of the sin, and seeking by the Holy Spirit to mortify the member in which the lust doth dwell. Did you lose Christ by neglecting the Scriptures? You must find Him in the Scriptures. It is a true proverb, "Look for a thing where you dropped it; it is there." So look for Christ where you lost Him, for He has not gone away. *Spurgeon*

March 16

Come behind in no gift. 1 Corinthians 1:7

The Scripture gives four names to Christians, taken from the four cardinal graces so essential to man's salvation: *Saints* for their holiness, *believers* for their faith, *brethren* for their love, *disciples* for their knowledge.
Thomas Fuller

March 17

They rest not day and night. Revelation 4:8

O blessed rest! When we rest not day and night, saying, "Holy, holy, holy, Lord God Almighty!"—when we shall rest from sin, but not from worship; from suffering and sorrow, but not from joy! O blessed day, when I shall rest with God; when I shall rest in knowing, loving, rejoicing, and praising; when my perfect soul and body shall together perfectly enjoy the most perfect God; when God, who is love itself, shall perfectly love me, and rest in His love to me, and I shall rest in my love to Him; when He shall rejoice over me with joy, and joy over me with singing, and I shall rejoice in Him! *Baxter*

March 18

*They that wait upon the Lord shall renew
their strength; they shall mount up with wings
as eagles; they shall run and not be weary,
and they shall walk and not faint.*
Isaiah 40:31

The eagle that soars in the upper air does not
worry itself as to how it is to cross rivers.
Selected

March 19

Their eyes were holden.   Luke 24:16.

Their eyes were opened.   Luke 24:31

There is much precious significance in this.
The Lord is often present in our lives in things
that we do not dream possess any significance.
We are asking God about something which
needs His mighty working, and the very instrument by which He is to work is by our side,
perhaps for weeks and months and years all
unrecognized, until suddenly someday it grows
luminous and glorious with the very presence
of the Lord, and becomes the mighty instrument of His victorious working. He loves to
show His hand through the unexpected. Often
he keeps us from seeing His way until just
before He opens it, and then, immediately that
it is unfolded, we find that He was walking by
our side in the very thing, long before we even
suspected its meaning.   *A. B. Simpson*

March 20

*All things work together for good to them that
love God.*   Romans 8:28

If our circumstances find us in God, we shall find God in all our circumstances.   *Selected*

March 21

He leadeth me in the paths of righteousness for His name's sake.   Psalm 23:3

He always has a purpose in His leading. He knows where the bits of green pasture are, and He would lead His flock to these. The way may be rough, but it is the right way to the pasture. "Paths of righteousness" may not be straight paths, but they are paths that lead somewhere— to the right place. Many desert paths are illusive. They start out clear and plain, but soon they are lost in the sands. They go nowhere. But the paths of righteousness have a goal to which they unerringly lead.   *J. R. Miller*

March 22

He said, "O my Lord, send, I pray Thee, by the hand of him whom Thou wilt send."
Exodus 4:13

It was a very grudging assent. It was as much as to say, "Since Thou art determined to send me and I must undertake the mission, then let it be so; but I would that it might have been another, and I go because I am compelled." So often do we shrink back from the sacrifice or obligation to which God calls us that we think we are going to our doom. We seek every reason for evading the divine will, little realizing that He is forcing us out from our quiet homes into a career which includes, among other things, the song of victory on the banks of the Red Sea; the two lonely sojourns for forty days in converse with God; the shining face; the vision of glory; the burial by the hand of Michael; and the supreme honor of standing beside the Lord on the Transfiguration mount.   *F. B. Meyer*

March 23

See then that ye walk circumspectly.
Ephesians 5:15

There is no such thing as negative influence. We are all positive in the place we occupy, making the world better or making it worse.
T. DeWitt Talmage

March 24

She took for him an ark of bulrushes . . . and she laid it in the flags by the river's brink.
Exodus 2:3

The mother of Moses laid the ark in the flags by the river's brink. But before doing so, she laid it on the heart of God! She could not have laid it so courageously upon the Nile if she had not first devoutly laid it upon the care and love of God.

We are often surprised at the outward calmness of men who are called upon to do unpleasant and most trying deeds; but could we have seen them in secret, we should have known the moral preparation which they underwent before coming out to be seen by men. Be right in the sanctuary if you would be right in the marketplace. Be steadfast in prayer if you would be calm in affliction. Start your race from the throne of God itself if you would run well and win the prize. *Joseph Parker*

March 25

Bear ye one another's burdens, and so fulfill the law of Christ. Galatians 6:2

By lifting the burdens of others we lose our own. *Selected*

March 26

I have finished the work which Thou gavest me to do. John 17:4

Was the work of the Master indeed done? Was not its heaviest task yet to come? He had not yet met the dread hour of death. Why did He say that His work was done? It was because He knew that, when the will is given, the battle is ended. He was only in the shadows of the garden; but to conquer these shadows was already to conquer all. He who has willed to die has already triumphed over death. All that remains to Him is but the outer husk, the shell.

The cup which our Father giveth us to drink is a cup for the will. It is easy for the lips to drain it when once the heart has accepted it. Not on the heights of Calvary but in the shadows of Gethsemane is the cup presented; the act is easy after the choice. The real battlefield is in the silence of the spirit. Conquer there, and thou art crowned. *George Matheson*

March 27

A great multitude ... stood before the throne.
Revelation 7:9

A *station on the feet* in front of the throne in *heaven* is the effect of being often *on the knees before* the throne on *earth.*   *Selected*

March 28

God saw the light, that it was good; and God divided the light from the darkness.
Genesis 1:4

No sooner is there a good thing in the world than a *division is necessary.* Light and darkness have no communion; God has divided them, let us not confound them. Sons of light must not have fellowship with deeds, doctrines, or deceits of darkness. The children of the day must be sober, honest, and bold in their Lord's work, leaving the works of darkness to those who shall dwell in it forever.

We should by our distinct separation from the world divide the light from the darkness. In judgment, in action, in hearing, in teaching, in association, we must discern between the precious and the vile, and maintain the great distinction which the Lord made upon the world's first day.

O Lord Jesus, be Thou our light throughout the whole of this day, for Thy light is the light of men.   *Spurgeon*

March 29

The path of the just is as the shining light

*that shineth more and more unto the
perfect day.*   Proverbs 4:18

Have I begun this path of heavenly love and
knowledge now? Am I progressing in it? Do I
feel some dawnings of the heavenly light, ear-
nests and antepasts of the full day of glory? Let
all God's dealings serve to quicken me in my
way. Let every affection it may please Him to
send be as the moving pillar-cloud of old, beck-
oning me to move my tent onward, saying,
"Arise ye and depart, for this is not your rest."
Let me be often standing now on faith's lofty
eminences, looking for "the day of God"—the
rising sun which is to set no more in weeping
clouds. Wondrous progression! How will all
earth's learning, its boasted acquirements and
eagle-eyed philosophy, sink into the lispings of
very infancy in comparison with this manhood
of knowledge! Heaven will be the true *"Excel-
sior,"* its song *"a song of degrees,"* Jesus leading
His people from height to height of glory, and
saying, as He said to Nathaniel, *"Thou shalt see
GREATER things than these!"*   Macduff

March 30

*Take us the foxes, the little foxes, that spoil
the vineyards; for our vineyards are in
blossom.*   Song of Solomon 2:15 ERV

How numerous the little foxes are! Little
compromises with the world; disobedience to
the still, small voice in little things; little indul-
gences of the flesh to the neglect of duty; little
strokes of policy; doing evil in little things that

good may come; and the beauty and the fruitfulness of the vine are sacrificed!
J. Hudson Taylor

March 31

*The children of your Father which is in
heaven.*   Matthew 5:45

The best name by which we can think of God
is Father. It is a loving, deep, sweet, heart-
touching name, for the name of father is in its
nature full of inborn sweetness and comfort.
Therefore also we must confess ourselves children of God, for by this name we deeply touch
our God, since there is not a sweeter sound to
the father than the voice of the child.
Martin Luther

April

April 1

In the morning came the word of the Lord unto me. Ezekiel 12:8

A quiet hour spent alone with God at the beginning of the day is the best beginning for the toils and cares of active business. A brief season of prayer, looking above for wisdom and grace and strength, and seeking for an outpouring of the Holy Spirit, helps us to carry our religion into the business of the day. It brings joy and peace within the heart. And as we place all our concerns in the care and keeping of the Lord, faithfully striving to do His will, we have a joyful trust that however dark or discouraging events may appear, our Father's hand is guiding everything, and will give the wisest direction to all our toils.   *Selected*

April 2

The Lord God formed man out of the dust of the ground, and breathed into his nostrils the breath of life; and man became a living soul. Genesis 2:7

And so this soul of mine is a compound of two worlds—dust and deity! It touches the boundary line of two hemispheres. It is allied on one side to the divine; on the other, to the beast of the field. Its beginning is from beneath, but its culmination is from above; it is started from the dust of the ground, but it is finished in the breath of God.

My soul, art thou living up to thy twofold origin? Art thou remembering thy double parentage, and therefore thy double duty? Thou hast a duty to thy God, for His breath is in thee; thou hast a duty to the earth, for out of it wast thou taken. *George Matheson*

April 3

Always rejoicing. 2 Corinthians 6:10

No Christian can ever know what is meant by those two little words "always rejoicing" but the Christian who takes up his cross and follows Jesus. *W. Hay Aitken*

April 4

All the land which thou seest, to thee will I give it, and to thy seed forever. Genesis 13:15

God's promises are ever on the ascending scale. One leads up to another, fuller and more blessed than itself. In Mesopotamia God said, "I will show thee the land." At Bethel, "This is the land." Here, "I will give thee all the land, and children innumerable as the grains of sand." And we shall find even these eclipsed.

It is thus that God allures us to saintliness. Not giving anything till we have dared to act— that He may test us. Not giving everything at first—that He may not overwhelm us. And always keeping in hand an infinite reserve of blessing. Oh, the unexplored remainders of God! Who ever saw His last star? *F. B. Meyer*

April 5

That night they caught nothing.   John 21:3

God may let the sinful world succeed in their forbidden schemes, but, blessed be His name, He does not allow His chosen ones to prosper in the path which leads them out of His holy will! He has a storm to send after every Jonah, and an empty net for every unbelieving and inconsistent Simon.   *A. B. Simpson*

April 6

They made me keeper of the vineyards; but mine own vineyard have I not kept.
 Song of Solomon 1:6

Our attention is here drawn to a danger which is preeminently one of this day: The intense activity of our times may lead to zeal in service *to the neglect of personal communion;* but such neglect will not only lessen the value of the service but tend to incapacitate us for the highest services.   *J. Hudson Taylor*

April 7

We came unto the land whither thou sentest us...we saw the children of Anak there.
Numbers 13:27,28

It is when we are in the way of *duty* that we find *giants*. It was when Israel was going *forward* that the giants appeared. When they turned back into the wilderness they found none. *Selected*

April 8

Each one resembled the children of a king.
Judges 8:18

If the King is indeed near of kin to us, the royal likeness will be recognizable.
Frances Ridley Havergal

April 9

He maketh me to lie down in green pastures;
He leadeth me beside the still waters.
Psalm 23:2

This suggests the rest into which our Good Shepherd leads His flock. Life is not all toil. God gives us many quiet resting-places in our pilgrim way.

Night is one of these, when, after the day's toil, struggle, and exhaustion we are led aside, and the curtains are drawn to shut out the noise, and He giveth His beloved sleep, in sleep giving the wonderful blessings of renewal. The Sabbath is another of these quiet resting-places. God would have us drop our worldly tasks, and have a day for the refreshing of both body and soul. . . . Friendship's trysts are also quiet resting places, where heart may commune with heart, where Jesus comes unseen and gives His blessing. All ordinances of Christian worship— seasons of prayer and devotion, hours of communion with God—are quiet resting-places.

Far more than we are apt to realize do we need these silent times in our busy life, needing them all the more the busier the life may be.
J. R. Miller

April 10

A daily rate for every day.   2 Kings 25:30

One staff aids a traveler, but a bundle of staves is a heavy burden.   *Spurgeon*

April 11

Bear ye one another's burdens, and so fulfill the law of Christ.   Galatians 6:2

However perplexed you may at any hour become about some question of truth, one refuge and resource is always at hand: You can do something for someone besides yourself. At the times when you cannot see God, there is still open to you this sacred possibility, to *show* God; for it is the love and kindness of human hearts through which the divine reality comes home to men, whether they name it or not. Let this thought, then, stay with you: There may be times when you cannot *find* help, but there is no time when you cannot *give* help.
George Merriam

April 12

Work out your own salvation with fear and trembling, for it is God which worketh in you both to will and to do of His good pleasure.
Philippians 2:12,13

It is not your business and mine to study whether we shall get to heaven, or even to study whether we shall be good men; it is our business to study how we shall come into the midst of the purposes of God and have the unspeakable privilege in these few years of doing something of His work.   *Phillips Brooks*

April 13

God...hath shined in our hearts, to give the light of the knowledge of the glory of God in the face of Jesus Christ.   2 Corinthians 4:6

Christian! Rest not until thou knowest the full, the unbroken shining of God in thy heart. To this end, yield to every stirring of it that shows thee some unconquered and perhaps unconquerable evil. Just bring it to the light; let the light shine upon it, and shine it out. Wait upon the Lord more than watchers for the morning, for "the path of the just is as the shining light, shining more and more unto the perfect day." Count upon it that God wants to fill thee with the light of His glory; wait on Him more than watchers for the morning. "Wait, I say, on the Lord."   *Andrew Murray*

April 14

My soul, wait thou only upon God.
Psalm 62:5

Did it ever occur to you that if you do not hear God's answer to prayer, it may be not because He is dumb but because you are deaf? Not because He has no answer to give but because you have not been listening for it? We are so busy with our service, so busy with our work, and sometimes so busy with our praying that it does not occur to us to stop our own talking and listen if God has some answer to give us with "the still small voice"; to be passive, to be quiet, to do nothing, say nothing; in some true sense think nothing—simply to be receptive and waiting for the voice. "Wait thou only upon God," says the psalmist; and again, "Wait on the Lord." *Selected*

April 15

Could ye not watch with me one hour?
Matthew 26:40

Oh, ye who sigh and languish and mourn your lack of power,
Heed ye this gentle whisper: "Could ye not watch one hour?"
To fruitfulness and blessing there is no "royal road";
The power for holy service is intercourse with God. *Selected*

April 16

My meat is to do the will of Him that sent me.
John 4:34

Seek your life's nourishment in your life's work. *Phillips Brooks*

April 17

It is God which worketh in you, both to will and to do of His good pleasure.
Philippians 2:13

Full salvation is to realize that everything we see in Christ, our Example, may be ours not by imitation but by reproduction. *Selected*

April 18

Lo, I am with you all the days.
Matthew 28:20 ERV margin

"ALL THE DAYS"—in winter days, when joys are fled; in sunless days, when the clouds return again and again after rain; in days of sickness and pain; in days of temptation and perplexity, as much as in days when the heart is as full of joy as the woodlands in spring are full of song. That day never comes when the Lord Jesus is not at the side of His saints. Lover and friend may stand afar, but He walks with them through the fires; He fords with them the rivers; He stands by them when face-to-face with the lion. We can never be alone. We must always add His resources to our own when making our calculations.   *F. B. Meyer*

April 19

Having . . . boldness to enter into the holiest by the blood of Jesus . . . let us draw near with a true heart.   Hebrews 10:19,22

Oh, the glory of the message! For fifteen centuries Israel had a sanctuary with a Holiest of All, into which, under pain of death, no one might enter. Its one witness was: Man cannot dwell in God's presence, cannot abide in His fellowship. And now how changed is all! As then the warning sounded, "No admittance! enter not!" so now the call goes forth, "Enter in! the veil is rent; the Holiest is open; God waits to welcome you to His bosom; henceforth you are to live with Him." This is the message. Child,

thy Father longs for thee to enter, to dwell, and
to go out no more forever.
Andrew Murray

April 20

*There stood by me this night the angel of
God...saying, "Fear not, Paul....God hath
given thee all them that sail with thee."
Wherefore...be of good cheer, for I believe
God, that it shall be even as it was told me.*
Acts 27:23-25

An active faith can give thanks for a promise,
though it be not yet performed, knowing that
God's bonds are as good as ready money.
Matthew Henry

April 21

*In everything by prayer and supplication, with
thanksgiving, let your requests be made known
unto God.*   Philippians 4:6

The natural temptation with every difficulty
is to plan for it, to put it out of the way yourself.
But stop short with all your planning, your
thinking, your worry, and talk to Him! "Cast thy
burden upon the Lord, and He shall sustain
thee." You may not always be able to do this in a
moment or two. Then keep on with supplication until you know He has it, and prayer
becomes praise. Rest, trust, and wait, and see
how He does that which you wanted to do, and
had so much care about. "Stand still and see the
salvation of the Lord."   *A. E. Funk*

April 22

They that wait upon the Lord shall...mount up with wings as eagles. Isaiah 40:31

All creatures that have wings can escape from every snare that is set for them, if only they will fly high enough; and the soul that uses its wings can always find a sure "way to escape" from all that can hurt or trouble it. *Smith*

April 23

Perfect love casteth out fear. 1 John 4:18

Fear and love rise up in antagonism to each other as motives in life, like those two mountains from which respectively the blessings and curses of the old law were pronounced—the Mount of Cursing all barren, stony, without verdure and without water; the Mount of Blessing green and bright with many a flower, and blessed with many a trickling rill. Fear is barren. Love is fruitful. The one is a slave, and its work is little worth. The other is free, and its deeds are great and precious. From the blasted summit of the mountain which gendereth to bondage may be heard the words of the law; but the power to keep all these laws must be sought on the sunny hill where liberty dwells in love and gives energy to obedience. Therefore, if you would use in your own life the highest power that God has given us for our growth in grace, draw your arguments not from fear but from love. *Alexander Maclaren*

April 24

The love of Christ constraineth us.
2 Corinthians 5:14

The love of Christ is too large for any heart to hold it. It will overflow into others' hearts; it will give itself out, give itself away, for the enriching of other lives. The heart of Christ is a costly thing for anyone to have. It will lead those who have it where it led Him. If it cost Him the cross, it will cost them no less.   *J. M. Campbell*

April 25

I the Lord thy God will hold thy right hand, saying unto thee, "Fear not; I will help thee."
Isaiah 41:13

Don't try to hold God's hand; let Him hold yours. Let Him do the *holding,* and you do the *trusting.*   *H. W. Webb-Peploe*

April 26

Consider how great things He hath done for you.   1 Samuel 12:24

Look back on all the way the Lord your God has led you. Do you not see it dotted with ten thousand blessings in disguise? Call to mind the needed succor sent at the critical moment; the right way chosen for you instead of the wrong way you had chosen for yourself; the hurtful thing to which your heart so fondly clung, removed out of your path; the breathing-time granted, which your tried and struggling spirit just at the moment needed. Oh, has not Jesus stood at your side when you knew it not? Has not Infinite Love encircled every event with its everlasting arms, and gilded every cloud with its merciful lining? Oh, retrace your steps, and mark His footprint in each one! Thank Him for them all, and learn the needed lesson of leaning more simply on Jesus.   *F. Whitfield*

April 27

He...said... "I...hid thy talent in the earth." ...His Lord answered and said unto him, "Thou wicked and slothful servant."
Matthew 25:24-26

Between the great things we cannot do and the small things we will not do, the danger is that we shall do nothing.   *Monod*

April 28

To Him be glory both now and forever.
2 Peter 3:18

Believer, you are anticipating the time when you shall join the saints above in ascribing all glory to Jesus; but are you glorifying Him *now*? The apostle's words are, "To Him be glory both *now* and forever."   *C. H. Spurgeon*

April 29

Thou shalt know that I am the Lord, for they shall not be ashamed that wait for me.
Isaiah 49:23

Quiet waiting before God would save from many a mistake and from many a sorrow.
J. Hudson Taylor

April 30

Be it unto thee even as thou wilt.
Matthew 15:28

Oh, the victories of prayer! They are the mountaintops of the Bible. They take us back to the plains of Mamre, to the fords of Peniel, to the prison of Joseph, to the triumphs of Moses, to the transcendent victories of Joshua, to the deliverances of David, to the miracles of Elijah and Elisha, to the whole story of the Master's life, to the secret of Pentecost, to the keynote of Paul's unparalleled ministry, to the lives of saints and the deaths of martyrs, to all that is most sacred and sweet in the history of the church and the experience of the children of God. And when, for us, the last conflict shall have passed, and the footstool of prayer shall have given place to the harp of praise, the spots of time that shall be gilded with the most celestial and eternal radiance shall be those often linked with deepest sorrow and darkest night, over which we have the inscription "Jehovah-Shammah: The Lord was there!"

A. B. Simpson

May

May 1

Thou art my God; early will I seek Thee.
Psalm 63:1

In a world where there is so much to ruffle the spirit's plumes, how needful that entering into the secret of God's pavilion, which will alone bring it back to composure and peace! In a world where there is so much to sadden and depress, how blessed the communion with Him in whom is the one true source and fountain of all true gladness and abiding joy! In a world where so much is ever seeking to unhallow our spirits, to render them common and profane, how high the privilege of consecrating them anew in prayer to holiness and to God.
Archbishop Trench

May 2

In Him was life, and the life was the light of men. John 1:4.

Ye are the light of the world. Matthew 5:14

In the light we can walk and work. We walk in the light and become entirely children of light. We let our light, the light of God, shine, so that men may see our good works and glorify our Father in heaven. Gently, silently, lovingly, unceasingly we give ourselves to transmit the light and the love that God so unceasingly shines into us. Our one work is to wait, and admit, and then *transmit* the light of God in Christ. *Andrew Murray*

May 3

Be ye steadfast, unmovable, always abounding in the work of the Lord.   1 Corinthians 15:58

Activity in doing good is one recipe for being cheerful Christians; it is like exercise to the body, and it keeps the soul in health.
Bishop Ryle

May 4

Looking up to heaven He sighed.   Mark 7:34

Too often we sigh and look within; Jesus sighed and looked without. We sigh and look down; Jesus sighed and looked up. We sigh and look to earth; Jesus sighed and looked to heaven. We sigh and look to man; Jesus sighed and looked to God.   *Stork*

May 5

We glory in tribulations.   Romans 5:3

Have you ever thought that someday you will never have anything to try you or anybody to vex you again?   *A. B. Simpson*

May 6

Set your affection on things above, not on things on the earth.   Colossians 3:2

He who has his affections set on things above is like one who hangs on by the skies; having a secure hold of these he could say, though he saw the world roll away from beneath his feet, "My heart is fixed; my heart is fixed; O Lord, I will sing and give praise!"   *Guthrie*

May 7

The Lord is risen indeed, and hath appeared to Simon.   Luke 24:34

They . . . gladly received [Peter's] word; and the same day there were added unto them about three thousand souls.   Acts 2:41

Before the Lord can use us in His service we must have close individual dealing with Himself. He always will have to do in *secret* with that soul that He intends to use in blessing others.

Do you want to speak for Jesus to those around you? Then you must go to Jesus Himself for your message. What you say *for* Jesus must come *from* Jesus.

Oh, how much breath falls powerless on every side because it has not been inhaled in the sanctuary! We want more secret dealing with the living God. We run without being sent; we speak before God has spoken to us. No wonder we so often fail! Oh, what secret prayer and what heart-searching discipline the heart needs before God can use it!   *F. Whitfield*

May 8

The righteous eateth to the satisfying of his soul.   Proverbs 13:25

Christ *must* satisfy. If we are not satisfied, it must be because we are not feeding on Him wholly and only. The fault is not in the provision which is made.   *Frances Ridley Havergal*

May 9

Whom the Lord loveth He chasteneth.
Hebrews 12:6

It has been well said that "earthly cares are a heavenly discipline," but they are even something better than discipline; they are God's chariots, sent to take the soul to its high places of triumph. In the Canticles we are told of "a chariot paved with love." We cannot always see the love lining to our own particular chariot—it often looks very unlovely; but every chariot sent by God must necessarily be paved with love, since God is love. It is His love, indeed, that sends the chariot.

Look upon your chastenings, then, no matter how grievous they may be for the present, as God's chariots, sent to carry your souls into the "high places" of spiritual achievement and uplifting, and you will find that they are, after all, "paved with love."   *Smith*

May 10

The blood of Jesus Christ, His Son, cleanseth us from all sin.   1 John 1:7

Learn a lesson from the eye of the miner, who all day long is working amid the flying coal dust. When he emerges in the light of day his face may be grimy enough; but his eyes are clear and lustrous, because the fountain of tears in the lachrymal gland is ever pouring its gentle tides over the eye, cleansing away each speck of dust as soon as it alights.

Is not this the miracle of cleansing which our spirits need in such a world as this? And this is what our blessed Lord is prepared to do for us by His cleansing blood, if only we will trust Him.   *F. B. Meyer*

May 11

Whatsoever He sayeth unto you, do it.
John 2:5

If I could give you information of my life, it would be to show how a woman of very ordinary ability has been led by God in strange and unaccustomed paths to do in His service what He has done in her. And if I could tell you all, you would see how God has done all, and I nothing. I have worked hard, very hard, that is all; and I have never refused God anything.
Florence Nightingale

May 12

I know how to abound.   Philippians 4:12

It is a dangerous thing to be prosperous. The crucible of adversity is a less severe trial to the Christian than the refining-pot of prosperity. It needs more than human skill to carry the brimming cup of mortal joy with a steady hand; yet Paul had learned that skill, for he declares, "In all things I am instructed both to be full and to be hungry." When we have much of God's providential mercies it often happens that we have but little of God's grace; satisfied with earth, we are content to do without heaven. Rest assured, it is harder to know how to be full than it is to know how to be hungry; so desperate is the tendency of human nature to pride and forget-fulness of God. Take care that you ask in your prayers that God would teach you "how to be full." *Spurgeon*

May 13

Whosoever exalteth himself shall be abased, and he that humbleth himself shall be exalted.
Luke 14:11

If you ask the way to the crown, 'tis by the cross; to the mountain, 'tis by the valley; to exaltation, 'tis he that humbleth himself.
J. H. Evans

May 14

For their sakes I sanctify myself, that they also might be sanctified through the truth.
John 17:19

Do you remember, when Jesus was sitting with His disciples at the last supper, how He lifted up His voice and prayed, and in the midst of His prayer there came these wondrous words: "For their sakes I sanctify myself, that they also might be sanctified"? Is there anything in all the teachings that man has had from the lips of God that is nobler, that is more far-reaching than that—to be my best not simply for my own sake but for the sake of the world? You can help your fellowmen, and you must help your fellow-men, but the only way you can help them is by being the noblest and the best man that it is possible for you to be. *Phillips Brooks*

May 15

He that is slow to anger is better than the mighty, and he that ruleth his spirit than he that taketh a city. Proverbs 16:32

More dear in the sight of God and His angels than any other conquest is the conquest of self, which each man, with the help of heaven, can secure for himself. *Dean Stanley*

May 16

For this child I prayed, and the Lord hath given me my petition which I asked of Him; therefore also I have lent him to the Lord: As long as he liveth he shall be lent to the Lord. 1 Samuel 1:27,28

God sometimes bestows gifts just that love may have something to renounce. The things that He puts into our hands are possibly put there that we may have the opportunity of showing what is in our heart. Oh, that there were in us a fervor of love that would lead us to examine everything that belongs to us, to ascertain how it might be made a means of showing our affection to Christ! *George Bowen*

May 17

Seek ye first the kingdom of God and His righteousness, and all these things shall be added unto you. Matthew 6:33

We need have only one care: that we put the first thing first—faithfulness to God. Then all else we need for both worlds will be supplied.

God will never fail us, but we sometimes forget in our rejoicing over such an assurance that we must fulfill our part if we would claim the divine promise.

It will not always be easy. Tomorrow it may mean a distasteful task, a disagreeable duty, a costly sacrifice for one who does not seem worthy. Life is full of sore testings of our willingness to follow the Good Shepherd. We have not the slightest right to claim this assurance unless we have taken Christ as the guide of our life.   *J. R. Miller*

May 18

His praise shall continually be in my mouth.
Psalm 34:1

Let not thy praises be transient—a fit of music, and then the instrument hung by the wall till another gaudy day of some remarkable providence makes thee take it down. God comes not guestwise to His saints' house, but to *dwell* with them. David took this up for a life work: "As long as I live, I will praise thee."
Gurnall

May 19

I am not able to bear all this people alone, because it is too heavy for me.
Numbers 11:14

It is most needful for all servants of Christ to remember that whenever the Lord places a man in a position of responsibility, He will both fit him for it and maintain him in it.

It is, of course, another thing altogether if a man will rush unsent into any field of work, or any post of difficulty or danger. In such a case we may assuredly look for a thorough break-down, sooner or later. But when God calls a man to a certain position, he will endow him with the needed grace to occupy it.

This holds good in every case. We can never fail if we only cling to the living God. We can never run dry if we are drawing from the fountain. Our tiny springs will soon dry up; but our Lord Jesus Christ declares, "He that believeth in me, as the Scripture hath said, out of his belly shall flow rivers of living water."
C. H. Mackintosh

May 20

Then said I, "Woe is me, for I am undone, because I am a man of unclean lips, and I dwell in the midst of a people of unclean lips; for mine eyes have seen the King, the Lord of hosts." Isaiah 6:5

It is not the sight of our sinful heart that humbles us; it is a sight of Jesus Christ. I am undone because mine eyes have seen the King.
Andrew A. Bonar

May 21

While I was musing the fire burned.
Psalm 34:3

My soul, if thou wouldst muse more, the fire would burn more. Why dost thou not retire oftener with thyself? Thou wouldst be better fitted for the world if thou wert less worldly. If thou hadst more heavenly fire thou wouldst have more earthly power.

Is there no secret pavilion into which thou canst go and warm thyself? Is there no holy of holies where thou canst catch a glow of impulse that will make thee strong? Is it not written of the Son of Man that "as He *prayed* the fashion of His countenance was altered"? Yes, it was from His prayer that His transfigured glory came. It was from the glow of His heart that there issued the glow of His countenance. It was when He was musing that the fire kindled.

O my soul, wouldst thou have thy life glorified, beautified, transfigured to the eyes of men? Get thee up into the secret place of God's pavilion, where the fires of love are burning. Thy life shall shine gloriously to the dwellers on the plain. Thy prayers shall be luminous; they shall light thy face like the face of Moses when he wist not that it shone. Thy words shall be burning; they will kindle many a heart journeying on the road to Emmaus. Thy path shall be radiant; when thou has prayed in Elijah's solitude thou shalt have Elijah's chariot of fire.

George Matheson

May 22

Whosoever shall give to drink unto one of these little ones a cup of cold water only in the name of a disciple, verily I say unto you, he shall in no wise lose his reward.
Matthew 10:42

We are in danger of looking too far for opportunities of doing good and communicating.

In reaching for rhododendrons we trample down the daisies.   *Selected*

May 23

Hide thyself by the brook.   1 Kings 17:3

Not by the *river*, but by the *brook*. The river would always contain an abundant supply, but the brook might dry up at any moment.

What does this teach us? God does not place His people in luxuriance here. The world's abundance might withdraw their affections from Him. He gives them not the river, but the brook. The brook may be running today, but tomorrow it may be dried up.

And wherefore does God act thus? To teach us that we are not to rest in His gifts and blessings, but in Himself. This is what our hearts are always doing—resting in the gift instead of the Giver. Therefore God cannot trust us by the river, for it unconsciously takes up His place in the heart. It is said of Israel that when they were full they forgot God.   *F. Whitfield*

May 24

His kingdom ruleth over all.   Psalm 103:19

His kingdom ruleth over all—therefore thou canst find nothing which is not matter for praise, since there is nothing which is not the matter of thy Lord's gracious permission, or planning, or control. *Over all*—nowhere canst thou step outside His realm, nor in anything get beyond His care and government. *Over all*—therefore take all as from God; hold all as from

God; and by thy gratitude give all back to God again, and thus complete the circle, making Him the Alpha and Omega, the Beginning and Ending of all things. *Mark Guy Pearse*

May 25

If we suffer we shall also reign with Him.
2 Timothy 2:12

The highest bidder for the crown of glory is the lowliest wearer of the cross of self-denial.
A. J. Gordon

May 26

Keep thy heart with all diligence, for out of it are the issues of life. Proverbs 4:23

He who would keep his heart pure and holy must plant a sentinel at every avenue by which sin may find access there, guarding against none more than the "little" sins, as they are called.

The man of God has his *eyes* to keep, and so Job said, "I have made a covenant with mine eyes," his *tongue,* and hence the exhortation, "Keep thy tongue from evil, and thy lips from speaking guile," his *ears,* and hence the warning, "Cease, my son, to hear the instruction that causeth to err," his *feet,* and hence David says, "I have refrained my feet from every evil way, that I might keep Thy word." And since there is no gate of the five senses by which the enemy may not come in like a flood unless the Spirit lift up a standard against him, we have need to guard every port and write over every portal, "Here

there entereth nothing to hurt or to defile."
Guthrie

May 27

Whatsoever ye do . . . do all in the name of the Lord Jesus. Colossians 3:17

Do little things as if they were great, because of the majesty of the Lord Jesus Christ, who dwells in thee; and do great things as if they were little and easy, because of His omnipotence. *Pascal*

May 28

Him they compelled to bear His cross.
Matthew 27:32

There are many Christians of whom this is true. They are compelled to bear the cross, but how does it come? It comes by their running away from it. They make up their minds they won't have Christ's cross; and they find when the cross does come that it comes in a more terrible form, with a more crushing weight than ever it would have come had they only been content to submit themselves to the divine direction; for the cross has to come to all who are to be prepared for glory hereafter.
W. Hay Aitken

May 29

Our Lord Jesus Christ . . . gave Himself for our sins that He might deliver us from this present evil world. Galatians 1:4

Attachment to Christ is the only secret of detachment from the world. *A. J. Gordon*

May 30

Ye are the light of the world. A city that is set on a hill cannot be hid.   Matthew 5:14

Lamps do not talk, but they do shine. A lighthouse sounds no drum, it beats no gong; and yet far over the waters its friendly spark is seen by the mariner. So let your actions shine out your religion. Let the main sermon of your life be illustrated by all your conduct.   *Spurgeon*

May 31

Without me ye can do nothing.   John 15:5

I can do all things through Christ who strengtheneth me.   Philippians 4:13

Apart from Him we can do nothing. While we are abiding in Him nothing is impossible. The one purpose of our life should therefore be to remain in living and intense union with Christ, guarding against everything that would break it, employing every means of cementing and enlarging it. And just in proportion as we do so, we shall find His strength flowing into us for every possible emergency. We may not feel its presence, but we shall find it present whenever we begin to draw on it. There is no temptation which we cannot master; no privation which we cannot patiently bear; no difficulty with which we cannot cope; no work which we cannot perform; no confession or testimony which we cannot make, if only our souls are living in healthy union with Jesus Christ; for as our day or hour, so shall our strength be.
F. B. Meyer

June

June 1

As my father hath sent me, even so send I you.
John 20:21

We should never leave our room until we have seen the face of our dear Master, Christ, and have realized that we are being sent forth by Him to do His will, and to finish the work which He has given us to do. He who said to His immediate followers, "As my Father hath sent me, even so send I you," says as much to each one of us, as the dawn summons us to live another day. We should realize that we are as much sent forth by Him as the angels who "do His commandments, hearkening unto the voice of His word." There is some plan for each day's work, which He will unfold to us if only we will look up to Him to do so; some mission to fulfill, some ministry to perform, some lesson patiently to learn, that we may be able to "reach others also." As to our plans we need not be anxious, because He who sends us forth is responsible to make the plan according to His infinite wisdom, and to reveal it to us, however dull and stupid our faculties may be. And as to our sufficiency, we are secure of having all needful grace, because He never sends us forth except He first breathes on us and says, "Receive ye the Holy Ghost." There is always a special endowment for special power.   *F. B. Meyer*

June 2

A fountain...for sin and for uncleanness.
Zechariah 13:1

You that have faith in the Fountain, *frequent it*. Beware of two errors which are very natural and very disastrous. Beware of thinking any sin too great for it; beware of thinking any sin too small. There is not a sin so little but it may be the germ of everlasting perdition; there is not a sin so enormous but a drop of atoning blood will wash it away as utterly as if it were drowned in the depths of the sea.   *James Hamilton*

June 3

I am my beloved's and his desire is toward me.
Song of Solomon 7:10

Nothing humbles the soul like sacred and intimate communion with the Lord; yet there is a sweet joy in feeling that *He* knows *all,* and notwithstanding loves us still.   *J. Hudson Taylor*

June 4

David inquired of the Lord.   2 Samuel 5:19

Christian, if thou wouldst know the path of duty, take God for thy compass; if thou wouldst steer thy ship through the dark billows, put the tiller into the hand of the Almighty. Many a rock might be escaped if we would let our Father take the helm; many a shoal or quicksand we might well avoid if we would leave it to His sovereign will to choose and to command. The Puritan said, "As sure as ever a Christian carves for himself he'll cut his own fingers." "I will instruct thee and teach thee in the way which thou shalt go" is God's promise to His people. Let us then take all our perplexities to

Him and say, "Lord, what wilt Thou have me to do?" Leave not thy chamber this morning without *inquiring of the Lord.*   *Spurgeon*

June 5

A certain man...who never had walked... heard Paul speak, who...perceiving that he had faith to be healed, said..."Stand upright on thy feet." And he leaped and walked.
Acts 14:8-10

Where true faith is, it will induce obedience; and where it does induce obedience, it will always, in one form or another, bring a blessing.
W. Hay Aitken

June 6

Then said Martha unto Jesus, "Lord...I know that...whatsoever Thou wilt ask of God, God will give it Thee." Jesus saith unto her, "Thy brother shall rise again." Martha saith unto Him, "I know that he shall rise again in the resurrection at the last day." John 11:21-24

In your prayer, beware above everything of limiting God, not only by unbelief but by fancying that you know what He can do. Expect unexpected things, *above all that* we ask or think. Each time you intercede, be quiet first and worship God in His glory. Think of what He can do, of how He delights to hear Christ, of your place in Christ; and expect great things.
Andrew Murray

June 7

As many of you as have been baptized into Christ have put on Christ. Galatians 3:27

Not simply the righteousness of our Savior, not simply the beauty of His holiness or the graces of His character, are we to put on as a garment. The Lord Himself is our vesture. Every Christian is not only a Christ-bearer but a Christ-wearer. We are so to enter into Him by communion, to be so endued with His presence, to be so embued with His Spirit that men shall see Him when they behold us, as they see our garments when they look upon our bodies. *A. J. Gordon*

June 8

Thou shalt never wash my feet. John 13:8

Whatever hinders us from receiving a blessing that God is willing to bestow upon us is not humility but the mockery of it. A genuine humility will ever feel the need of the largest measures of grace, and will be perfected just in the degree in which that grace is bestowed. The truly humble man will seek to be filled with all the fullness of God, knowing that when so filled there is not the slightest place for pride or for self. *George Bowen*

June 9

Cast thy burden upon the Lord, and He shall sustain thee. Psalm 55:22

He that taketh his own cares upon himself loads himself with an uneasy burden. The fear of what *may* come, the expectation of what *will* come, the desire of what will *not* come, and the inability to redress all these must needs bring him continual torment. *I* will cast my cares upon *God:* He hath bidden me. They cannot hurt Him: He can redress them.   *Hall*

June 10

Well done, good and faithful servant....
Thou wicked and slothful servant.
Matthew 25:21,26

God holds us responsible not for what we *have* but for what we *might have*; not for what we *are* but for what we *might be*.   *Mark Guy Pearse*

June 11

Jesus constrained His disciples to get into
a ship.   Matthew 14:22

Jesus *constrained* them to go! One would think that if ever there was the certain promise of success in a mission, it was here. Surely here, if anywhere, a triumphant issue might have been confidently predicted; and yet here, more than anywhere, there was seeming failure. He sent them out on a voyage, and they met such a storm as they had never yet experienced.

Let me ponder this, for it has been so with me, too. I have sometimes felt myself impelled to act by an influence which seemed above me—constrained to put to sea. The belief that I was constrained gave me confidence, and I was sure of a calm voyage. But the result was outward failure. The calm became a storm; the sea raged, the winds roared, the ship tossed in the midst of the waves, and my enterprise was wrecked ere it could reach the land.

Was then my divine command a delusion?

Nay; nor yet was my mission a failure. He did send me on that voyage, but He did not send me for *my* purpose. He had one end and I had another. My end was the outward calm; His was my meeting with the storm. My end was to gain the harbor of a material rest; His was to teach me there is a rest even on the open sea.
George Matheson

June 12

Study to show thyself approved unto God, a workman that needeth not to be ashamed, rightly dividing the word of truth.
2 Timothy 2:15

Have thy tools ready; God will find thee work.   *Charles Kingsley*

June 13

Come out from among them, and be ye separate.   2 Corinthians 6:17

With all the world in His choice, God placed His ancient people in a very remarkable situation. On the north they were walled in by the snowy ranges of Lebanon; a barren desert formed their eastern boundary; far to the south stretched a sterile region, called the howling wilderness; while the sea—not then, as now, the highway of the nations, facilitating rather than impeding intercourse—lay on their west, breaking

on a shore that had few harbors and no naviga-
ble rivers to invite the steps of commerce.

May we not find a great truth in the very
position in which God placed His chosen people?
It certainly teaches us that to be holy, or sanctified, we must be a separate people—living in
the world, but not of it—as oil, that may be
mixed but cannot be combined with water.
Guthrie

June 14

*I am with thee, and will keep thee in all places
whither thou goest, and will bring thee again
into this land.*   Genesis 28:15

"With thee," companionship; "keep thee,"
guardianship; "bring thee," guidance.

June 15

*I have set thee . . . that thou shouldst be for
salvation unto the ends of the earth.*
Acts 13:37

*Ye shall be witnesses unto me . . . unto the
uttermost parts of the earth.*   Acts 1:8

Men are questioning now, as they never have
questioned before, whether Christianity is indeed the true religion which is to be the salvation of the world. Christian men, it is for us to
give our bit of answer to that question. It is for
us, in whom the Christian church is at this
moment partially embodied, to declare that
Christianity, that the Christian faith, the Christian manhood can do that for the world which
the world needs.

You ask, "What can I do?"

You can furnish one Christian life. You can furnish a life so faithful to every duty, so ready for every service, so determined not to commit every sin that the great Christian church shall be the stronger for your living in it, and the problem of the world be answered, and a certain great peace come into this poor, perplexed, phase of our humanity as it sees that new revelation of what Christianity is.   *Phillips Brooks*

June 16

I know whom I have believed.   2 Timothy 1:12

Personal acquaintance with Christ is a living thing. Like a tree that uses every hour for growth, it thrives in sunshine, it is refreshed by rain—even the storm drives it to fasten its grip more firmly in the earth for its support. So, troubled heart, in all experience, say, "This comes that I may make closer acquaintance with my Lord."   *Selected*

June 17

Wait for the promise of the Father.   Acts 1:4

When the day of Pentecost was fully come, they were all with one accord in one place . . . and they were all filled with the Holy Ghost.
Acts 2:1,4

Obedience to a divine prompting transforms it into a permanent acquisition.   *F. B. Meyer*

June 18

We have known and believed the love that God hath to us.   1 John 4:16

The secret of walking closely with Christ, and working successfully for Him is to fully realize that we are His beloved. Let us but feel that He has set His heart upon us, that He is watching us from those heavens with tender interest, that He is working out the mystery of our lives with solicitude and fondness, that He is following us day by day as a mother follows her babe in his first attempt to walk alone, that He has set His love upon us, and, in spite of ourselves, is working out for us His highest will and blessing, as far as we will let Him, and then nothing can discourage us. Our hearts will glow with responsive love. Our faith will spring to meet His mighty promises, and our sacrifices shall become the very luxuries of love for one so dear. This was the secret of John's spirit. "We have known and believed the love that God hath to us." And the heart that has fully learned this has found the secret of unbounded faith and enthusiastic service.   *A. B. Simpson*

June 19

Endure . . . as a good soldier of Jesus Christ.
2 Timothy 2:3

Life is not victory, but battle. Be patient a little longer. By and by, each in his turn, we shall hear the sunset gun.   *Selected*

June 20

Whosoever doth not bear his cross and come after me cannot be my disciple.   Luke 14:27

There is always the shadow of the cross resting upon the Christian's path. Is that a reason why you should avoid or not undertake the duty? Have you made up your mind that you will follow your Master everywhere else, save when He ascends the path that leads to the cross? Is that your religion? The sooner you change it, the better. The religion of the Lord Jesus Christ is the religion of the cross, and unless we take up our cross, we can never follow Him.   *W. Hay Aitken*

June 21

These...have turned the world upside down. Acts 17:6

The serene beauty of a holy life is the most powerful influence in the world next to the might of God.   *Pascal*

June 22

What I do thou knowest not now, but thou shalt know hereafter.   John 13:7

God keeps a school for His children here on earth, and one of His best teachers is Disappointment. My friend, when you and I reach our Father's house, we shall look back and see that the sharp-voiced, rough-visaged teacher, Disappointment, was one of the best guides to train us for it. He gave us hard lessons; he often used the rod; he often led us into thorny paths; he sometimes strips off a load of luxuries; but that only made us travel the freer and the faster on our heavenward way. He sometimes led us down into the valley of the death-shadow; but never did the promises read so sweetly as when spelled out by the eye of faith in that very valley. Nowhere did he lead us so often, or teach us such sacred lessons, as at the cross of Christ. Dear, old, rough-handed teacher! We will build a monument to thee yet, and crown it with garlands, and inscribe on it: *Blessed be the memory of Disappointment!* *Theodore Cuyler*

June 23

As thy days, so shall thy strength be.
Deuteronomy 23:25.

I can do all things through Christ who strengtheneth me. Philippians 4:13

He will not impose upon you one needless burden. He will not exact more than He knows your strength will bear. He will ask no Peter to come to Him on the water unless He impart at the same time strength and support on the unstable waves. He will not ask you to draw water if the well is too deep, or to withdraw the stone if too heavy. But neither at the same time will He admit as an impossibility that which, as a free and responsible agent, it is in your power to avert. He will not regard as your misfortune what is your crime. *Macduff*

June 24

Thy heart is not right in the sight of God.
Acts 8:21

The worst of all mockeries is a religion that leaves the heart unchanged: a religion that has *everything* but the love of Christ enshrined in the soul.   *F. Whitfield*

June 25

The Holy Ghost said, "Separate me Barnabas and Saul for the work whereunto I have called them." Acts 13:2

We have such a nice little quiet, shady corner in the vineyard, down among the tender grapes, with such easy little weedings and waterings to attend to. And then the Master comes and draws us out into the thick of the work, and puts us in a part of the field where we never would have thought of going, and puts larger tools into our hands, that we may do more at a stroke. And we know we are not sufficient for these things, and the very tools seem too heavy for us, and the glare too dazzling and the vines too tall. But would we dally and go back? He would not then be in the shady corner with us; for when He put us forth He went before us, and it is only by closely following that we can abide with Him. *Frances Ridley Havergal*

June 26

Small things.   Zechariah 4:10

It is the little words you speak, the little thoughts you think, the little things you do or leave undone, the little moments you waste or use wisely, the little temptations which you yield to or overcome—the little things of every day

that are making or marring your future life.
Selected

June 27

Be perfect, be of good comfort.
2 Corinthians 13:11

A glance at the words is enough to make us feel how contradictory they are. *Be perfect*—that is a word that strikes us with despair; at once we feel how far away we are from our own poor ideal, and how much further yet from God's ideal concerning us. *Be of good comfort*—ah, that is very different! That seems to say, "Do not fret; do not fear. If you are not what you would be, but you must be thankful for what you are."

Now the question is this: How can these two be reconciled?

It is only the religion of Jesus Christ that reconciles them. He stands in our midst, and with the right hand of His righteousness He pointeth us upward and saith, "Be perfect." There is no resting place short of that. Yet with the left hand of His love He doth encompass us as He saith, "Soul, be of good comfort; for that is what I came to do for thee." *Mark Guy Pearse*

June 28

Be ye therefore perfect, even as your Father who is in heaven is perfect. Matthew 5:48

Seeking the aid of the Holy Spirit, let us aim at perfection. Let every day see some sin crucified, some battle fought, some good done, some victory won; let every fall be followed by a rise, and every step gained become not a resting-place but a new starting-point for further and higher progress. *Guthrie*

June 29

Sleep on now, and take your rest. Mark 14:41

Never did that sacred opportunity to watch with Christ return to His disciples. Lost then, it was lost forever. And now when Jesus is still beholding the travail of His soul in the redemption of the world, if you fail to be with Him watching for souls as they that must give account, remember that the opportunity will never return. "Watch, therefore," says your Lord, "lest coming suddenly, He may find you sleeping." *A. J. Gordon*

June 30

Let us not sleep, as do others.
1 Thessalonians 5:6

There are many ways of promoting Christian wakefulness. Among the rest, let me strongly advise Christians to converse together concerning the ways of the Lord. Christian and Hopeful, as they journeyed toward the Celestial City, said to themselves:

"To prevent drowsiness in this place, let us fall into good discourse."

Christians who isolate themselves and walk alone are very liable to grow drowsy. Hold Christian company, and you will be kept wakeful by it, and refreshed and encouraged to make quicker progress in the road to heaven.
Spurgeon

July

July 1

He laid His right hand upon me, saying unto me, "Fear not." Revelation 1:17

One of Wellington's officers, when commanded to go on some perilous duty, lingered a moment as if afraid, and then said:

"Let me have one clasp of your all-conquering hand before I go, and then I can do it."

Seek the clasp of Christ's hand before every bit of work, every hard task, every battle, every good deed. Bend your head in the dewy freshness of every morning, ere you go forth to meet the day's duties and perils, and wait for the benediction of Christ as He lays His hands upon you. They are hands of blessing. Their touch will inspire you for courage and strength and all beautiful and noble living. *J. R. Miller*

July 2

Being seen of them forty days, and speaking of the things pertaining to the kingdom of God. Acts 1:3

This lingering for forty days is the crowning proof of Christ's tender regard for His little flock. He who had laid down His life for them is loath to leave them. Though they had forsaken Him and doubted Him, they had not wearied, much less had they worn out, His love. He stays to look again, and yet again, and yet again, upon them, as if turning back and lingering to bless them. It is all of a piece with His life of love. Everywhere He meets them without a touch of upbraiding, without recalling a single memory of all His bitter suffering, revealing Himself to the disciples with a tenderness and blessedness indescribably beautiful.

How can He go till He has healed the Magdalene's broken heart? He must linger till poor Peter can venture near to have his forgiveness assured. He must stay to strengthen Thomas' faith. He must tarry with them till He has made them feel that He is just the same friendly, brotherly Jesus that He has ever been, caring for them in their work, watching them with a yearning pity, stooping to kindle a fire for their warmth, and to cook the fish for their meal, and then to bid them come and dine.

Mark Guy Pearse

July 3

Jesus . . . being wearied with His journey, sat thus on the well. . . . (For His disciples were gone away unto the city to buy meat.) . . . And many of the Samaritans of that city believed on Him for the saying of the woman, which testified, "He told me all that ever I did."
John 4:6,8,39

The bits of wayside work are very sweet. Perhaps the odd bits, when all is done, will really come to more than the seemingly greater pieces! . . . It is nice to know that the King's servants are always really on duty, even while some can only stand and wait.

Frances Ridley Havergal

July 4

Peace I leave with you, my peace I give unto you....Let not your heart be troubled, neither let it be afraid. John 14:27

Dark hours come to us all; and if we have no firm cable to a peace that can pass unbroken through their murky gloom, we shall be in a state of continual dread. Any stone flung by a chance passerby may break the crystal clearness of the Lake of Peace and send disturbing ripples across it, unless we have learned to trust in the perpetual presence of Him who can make and keep a great calm within the soul. Only let nothing come to you which you shall not instantly hand over to Him—all petty worries, all crushing difficulties, all inability to believe.
F. B. Meyer

July 5

Isaac dwelt by the well Lahai-roi. Genesis 25:11

Isaac *dwelt* there, and made the well of the living and all-seeing God his constant source of supply. The usual tenor of a man's life, the *dwelling* of his soul, is the true test of his state. Let us learn to live in the presence of the living God. Let us pray the Holy Spirit that this day, and every other day, we may feel, "Thou God seest me." May the Lord Jehovah be as a well to us— delightful, comforting, unfailing, springing up unto eternal life. The bottle of the creature cracks and dries up, but the well of the Creator never fails. Happy is he who dwells at the well, and so has abundant and constant supplies near at hand! Glorious Lord, constrain us that we may never leave Thee, but dwell by the well of the living God!   *Spurgeon*

July 6

Judas Iscariot...was a thief, and had the bag, and bore what was put therein.   John 12:4,6

Freely ye have received, freely give.
Matthew 10:8

If we should go thoroughly into this matter, should we not find that many of us are guilty, in some modified and yet sufficiently alarming sense, of treachery to the poor? Are we not, some of us, sent to them with benefactions which never reach them, and are only unconscious of guilt because so long accustomed to look upon the goods as bestowed on us, whereas the light of God's Word would plainly reveal upon those goods the names of the poor and needy?   *George Bowen*

July 7

Let every man take heed how he buildeth.
1 Corinthians 3:10

Our business is not to build quickly, but to build upon a right foundation, and in a right spirit. Life is more than a mere competition as between man and man; it is not who can be done first, but who can work best; it is not who can rise highest in the shortest time, but who is working most patiently and lovingly in accordance with the designs of God.   *Joseph Parker*

July 8

As thy days, so shall thy strength be.
Deuteronomy 33:25

No day without its duty; no duty without strength to perform it.   *Selected*

July 9

Surely the Lord is in this place, and I knew it not.   Genesis 28:16

"Surely the Lord was in this place, and I knew it not." My soul, this is also thine experience! How often hast thou said in thy sorrow, "Verily thou art a God that hidest Thyself!" How often hast thou slept for very heaviness of heart, and desired not to wake again! And when thou didst wake again, lo, the darkness was all a dream! Thy vision of yesterday was a delusion. God had been with thee all the night with that radiance which has no need of the sun.

O my soul, it is not only after the future thou must aspire; thou must aspire to see the glory of thy past. Thou must find the glory of that way by which thy God has led thee, and be able even of thy sorrow to say, "This was the gate of heaven!"   *George Matheson*

July 10

My meat is to do the will of Him that sent me.
John 4:34

The real secret of an unsatisfied life lies too often in an unsurrendered will.
J. Hudson Taylor

July 11

Giving all diligence, add to your faith virtue.
2 Peter 1:5

You will find it less easy to unroot faults than to choke them by gaining virtues. Do not think of your faults, still less of others' faults; in every person who comes near you look for what is good and strong; honor that; rejoice in it and as you can, try to imitate it; and your faults will drop off like dead leaves when their time comes.
John Ruskin

July 12

Awake, O north wind; and come, thou south; blow upon my garden, that the spices thereof may flow out.   Song of Solomon 4:16

Sometimes God sends severe blasts of trial upon His children to develop their graces. Just as torches burn most brightly when swung violently to and fro, just as the juniper plant smells sweetest when flung into the flames, so the richest qualities of a Christian often come out under the north wind of suffering and adversity. Bruised hearts often emit the fragrance that God loveth to smell. Almost every true believer's experience contains the record of trials which were sent for the purpose of shaking the spice tree.   *Theodore Cuyler*

July 13

Awake, O north wind; and come, thou south; blow upon my garden, that the spices thereof may flow out.   Song of Solomon 4:16

There are two winds mentioned in this beautiful prayer. God may send either or both as seemeth Him good. He may send the north wind of conviction, to bring us to repentance, or He may send the south wind of love, to melt us into gratitude and holy joy. If we often require the sharp blasts of trial to develop our graces, do we not also need the warm south breezes of His mercy? Do we not need the new sense of Christ's presence in our hearts and the joys of the Holy Ghost? Do we not need to be melted, yea, to be overpowered by the love of Jesus?
Theodore Cuyler

July 14

Behold the man! John 19:5

"Behold the man!" was Pilate's jeer. That is what all the ages have been doing since, and the vision has grown more and more glorious. As they have looked, the crown of thorns has become a crown of golden radiance, and the cast-off robe has glistened like the garments He wore on the night of the transfiguration. Martyrs have smiled in the flames at that vision. Sinners have turned at it to a new life. Little children have seen it, and have had awakened by it dim recollections of their heaven-home. Toward it the souls of men yearn ever.
Robert E. Speer

July 15

He [John] saith, "Behold the Lamb of God!" And the two disciples heard him speak, and they followed Jesus. John 1:36,37

To be a Christian means to know the presence of a true personal Christ among us, and to follow. *Phillips Brooks*

July 16

Ye shall not eat of it. Genesis 3:3

The sin of Paradise was eating the tree of knowledge before the tree of life. Life must ever be first. Knowing and not being, hearing and not doing, admiring and not possessing, all are light without life. *Selected*

July 17

Let patience have her perfect work, that ye may be perfect and entire, wanting nothing.
James 1:4

Are you where God would have you be? If not, come out, and at once, for you certainly ought not to be there. If you are, then be afraid to complain of circumstances which God has ordained on purpose to work out in you the very image and likeness of His son. *Mark Guy Pearse*

July 18

Sow beside all waters. Isaiah 32:20

Never mind where your work is. Never mind whether it be visible or not. Never mind whether your name is associated with it. You may never see the issues of your toils. You are working for eternity. If you cannot see results here in the hot working day, the cool evening hours are

drawing near, when you may rest from your labors and then they will follow you. So do your duty, and trust God to give the seed you sow "a body as it hath pleased Him."
Alexander Maclaren

July 19

Hold thou me up, and I shall be safe.
Psalm 119:117

Do not spoil the chime of this morning's bells by ringing only half a peal. Do not say, "Hold thou me up," and stop there, or add, "But all the same I shall stumble and fall!" Finish the peal with God's own music, the bright words of faith that He puts into your mouth: "Hold thou me up, *and I shall be safe!*"   *Frances Ridley Havergal*

July 20

Lord, my servant lieth at home sick of the palsy.   Matthew 8:6

We, in this age of the church, are in the position of that sick servant at Capernaum. To the eye of sense we are separated from the Savior. We see Him not; we can touch Him not; the hand cannot steal amid the crowd to catch His garment hem; we cannot hear His loved footsteps as of old on our threshold. But faith penetrates the invisible: The messenger—prayer—meets Him in the streets of the New Jerusalem; and faith and prayer together, the twin delegates from His church below, He has never yet sent away empty.   *Macduff*

July 21

Work out your own salvation with fear and trembling; for it is God which worketh in you both to will and to do of His good pleasure.
Philippians 2:12,13

What a staggering weight of thought is excited by these words! Stay, my soul, and wonder that the Eternal God should stoop to work within thy narrow limits. Is it not a marvel indeed that He whom the heavens cannot contain, and in whose sight they are not clean, should trouble Himself to work on material so unpromising and amidst circumstances so uncongenial?

How careful should we be to make Him welcome, and to throw no hindrance in His way! How eager to garner up all the least movements of His gracious operation, as the machinist conserves the force of his engine, and as the goldsmith with miserly care collects every flake of gold-leaf! Surely we shall be sensible of the *fear* of holy reverence and the *trembling* of eager anxiety as we "work out," into daily act and life, all that God our Father is "working in."
F. B. Meyer

July 22

...sinners, of whom I am chief....Now unto the King, eternal, immortal, invisible, the only wise God, be honor and glory for ever and ever. Amen. 1 Timothy 1:15,17

Only those who have struck the deepest note of penitence can reach the highest note of praise. *A. J. Gordon*

July 23

Blessed is the man . . . that keepeth the Sabbath.
Isaiah 56:2

The Sabbath is the savings bank of human life, into which we deposit one day in seven to be repaid in the autumn of life with compound interest.   *Selected*

July 24

Cleanse thou me from secret faults.
Psalm 19:12

The world wants men who are saved from secret faults. The world can put on an outside goodness and go very far in uprightness and morality, but it expects that a Christian shall go beyond this and be free from secret faults. A little crack will spoil the ring of the coin . . . . The world expects, and rightly, that the Christian should be more gentle and patient and generous than he who does not profess to be a disciple of the Lord Jesus. For the sake of those who take their notion of religion from our lives, we need to put up this prayer earnestly: "Cleanse thou me from secret faults."   *Mark Guy Pearse*

July 25

Do thou that which is good.   2 Kings 10:5

Keep as few good intentions hovering about as possible. They are like ghosts haunting a dwelling. The way to lay them is to find bodies for them. When they are embodied in substantial deeds they are no longer dangerous.
William Arnot

July 26

Grow in grace, and in the knowledge of our Lord and Savior, Jesus Christ. 2 Peter 3:18

Grace has its dawn as well as day; grace has its green blade, and afterward its ripe corn in the ear; grace has its babes and its men in Christ. With God's work there, as with all His works, "in all places of His dominion," progress is both the prelude and the path to perfection. Therefore we are exhorted to grow in grace, and in the knowledge of our Lord and Savior Jesus Christ, to go on to perfection, saying with Paul, "I count not myself to have apprehended; but this one thing I do, forgetting those things which are behind, and reaching forth unto those things which are before, I press toward the mark for the prize of the high calling of God in Christ Jesus." *Guthrie*

July 27

Sin, taking occasion by the commandment, deceived, and by it slew me. Romans 7:11

Christian, beware how thou thinkest lightly of sin. Take heed lest thou fall by little and little. Sin, a *little* thing? Is it not a poison? Who knows its deadliness? Sin, a little thing? Do not the little foxes spoil the grapes? Doth not the tiny coral insect build a rock which wrecks a navy? Do not little strokes fell lofty oaks? Will not continual drippings wear away stones? Sin, a little thing? It girded the Redeemer's head with thorns and pierced His heart! It made *Him* suffer anguish, bitterness, and woe. Could you weigh the least sin in the scales of eternity, you would fly from it as from a serpent, and abhor *the least appearance of evil.* Look upon all sin as that which crucified the Savior, and you will see it to be "exceeding sinful."   *Spurgeon*

July 28

Your heavenly Father knoweth.   Matthew 6:32

The Master judges by the result, but our Father judges by the effort. Failure does not always mean fault. He knows how much things cost, and weighs them where others only measure. Your Father! Think how great store His love sets by the poor beginnings of the little ones, clumsy and unmeaning as they may be to others. All this lies in this blessed relationship, and infinitely more. Do not fear to take it all as your own.   *Mark Guy Pearse*

July 29

Ye are dead, and your life is hid with Christ in God.   Colossians 3:3

It is neither talent nor power nor gifts that do the work of God, but it is that which lies within the power of the humblest: It is the simple earnest life hid with Christ in God.
F. W. Robertson

July 30

The mother of Jesus saith unto Him, "They have no wine." Jesus saith unto her, "Woman,

what have I to do with thee? Mine hour is not yet come." His mother saith unto the servants, "Whatsoever He saith unto you, do it."
John 2:3-5

In asking for temporal blessings, true wisdom lies in putting the matter into the Lord's hand and leaving it there. He knows our sorrows, and if He sees it is good for us that the water should be turned into wine, He will do it. It is not for us to dictate: He sees what is best for us. When we ask for prosperity, perhaps the thing which we should have is trial. When we want to be relieved of a "thorn in the flesh," He knows what we should have is an apprehension of the fact that His grace is sufficient for us. So we are put into His school, and have to learn the lessons He has to teach us.   *W. Hay Aitken*

July 31

Let him that thinketh he standeth take heed lest he fall.   1 Corinthians 10:12

Angels fell in heaven, Adam in paradise, Peter in Christ's presence.
Theophilus Polwheile

August

August 1
Continue in prayer.   Colossians 4:2

The greatest and the best talent that God gives to any man or woman in this world is the talent of prayer. And the best usury that any man or woman brings back to God when He comes to reckon with them at the end of this world is a life of prayer. And those servants best put their Lord's money to the exchangers who rise early and sit late as long as they are in this world, ever finding out and ever following after better and better methods of prayer, and ever forming more secret, more steadfast, and more spiritually fruitful habits of prayer, till they literally pray without ceasing, and till they continually strike out into new enterprises in prayer, and new achievements, and new enrichments.   *Alexander Whyte*

August 2
He entered into one of the ships . . . and . . . sat down.   Luke 5:8

When Jesus sits in the ship everything is in its right place. The cargo is in the hold, *not in the heart.* Cares and gains, fears and losses, yesterday's failure and today's success do not thrust themselves in between us and His presence. The heart cleaves to *Him.* "Goodness and mercy shall *follow* me," sang the psalmist. Alas, when the goodness and mercy come before us, and our blessings shut Jesus from view! Here is the blessed order: the Lord ever first, I following

Him, His goodness and mercy following me.
Mark Guy Pearse

August 3

Now are ye light in the Lord: walk as children of light.   Ephesians 5:8

We do not realize the importance of the unconscious part of our life ministry. It goes on continually. In every greeting we give to another on the street, in every moment's conversation, in every letter we write, in every contact with other lives, there is a subtle influence that goes from us that often reaches further, and leaves a deep impression than the things themselves that we are doing at the time. It is not so much what we *do* in this world as what we *are* that tells in spiritual results and impressions.
J. R. Miller

August 4

Created in Christ Jesus unto good works.
Ephesians 2:10

Let us ask Him to work in us to *will* those good works, so that our *will*, without being impaired in its free operation, may be permeated and molded by His will, just as light suffuses the atmosphere without displacing it. And let us also expect that He will infuse into us sufficient strength that we may be able to *do* His will unto all pleasing. Thus day by day our life will be a manifestation of those holy volitions and lovely deeds which shall attest the indwelling and inworking of God. And men shall see our good works, and glorify our Father who is in heaven. *F. B. Meyer*

August 5

Go in this thy might . . . have not I sent thee?
Judges 6:14

God never leaves His child to fail when in the path of obedience. *Theodore Cuyler*

August 6

Set your affection on things above, not on things on the earth. Colossians 3:2

Whatsoever thy hand findeth to do, do it with thy might. Ecclesiastes 9:10

If we are to live separate from the world, how, since men only do well what they do with a will, are we with affections fixed on things above to perform aright the secular, ordinary duties of life? If our hearts are engrossed with heavenly things, how are we to obey this other and equally divine commandment, "Whatsoever thy hand findeth to do, do it with thy might"?

The two are perfectly consistent. Man standing between the celestial and terrestrial worlds is related to both; he resembles neither a flower, which, springing from the dust and returning to it, belongs altogether to the earth, nor a star, which, shining far remote from its lower sphere, belongs altogether to the heavens. Our hearts may instead be likened to the rainbow, that, rising into heaven but resting on earth, is connected both with the clods of the valley and the clouds of the sky. *Guthrie*

August 7

Let us lay aside every weight, and the sin which doth so easily beset us, and let us run with patience the race that is set before us, looking unto Jesus. Hebrews 12:1,2

Think, as you sit here, of anything that you are doing that is wrong, of any habit of your life, of your self-indulgence, or of that great pervasive habit of your life which makes you a creature of the present instead of the eternities, a creature of the material earth instead of the glorious skies. Ask yourself of any habit that belongs to your own personal life, and bring it face-to-face with Jesus Christ. *Phillips Brooks*

August 8

They took knowledge of them, that they had been with Jesus. Acts 4:13

If I think of the world, I get the impress of the world; if I think of my trials and sorrows, I get the impress of my trials and sorrows; if I think of my failures, I get the impress of my failures; if I think of Christ, I get the impress of Christ. *Selected*

August 9

Ye call me Teacher and Lord, and ye say well, for so I am. John 13:13 ERV margin

How wonderful a Teacher we have! Sometimes we seek Him in the house, but He is not there. We go forth seeking Him and find Him perhaps in the wilderness or on a mountain praying, or leading some poor blind man by the hand or eating with publicans or sinners, or asleep in a storm or conversing with a Samaritan woman, or surrounded by wrathful men, or bearing a cross. It is not merely His words that instruct. His place, His occupation, His companions, His environment, His garment, His silence, His submission—all teem with instruction. And they that learn of Him are made like unto Him. *George Bowen*

August 10

The Father sent the Son to be the Savior of the world.   1 John 4:14

It is a sweet thought that Jesus Christ did not come forth without His Father's permission, authority, consent, and assistance. He was sent of the Father that He might be the Savior of men....Didst thou ever consider the depth of love in the heart of Jehovah, when God the Father equipped His Son for the great enterprise of mercy? If not, be this thy day's meditation. The *Father* sent Him! Contemplate that subject. Think how Jesus works what the *Father* wills. In the wounds of the dying Savior see the love of the great I AM. Let every thought of Jesus be also connected with the eternal, ever-blessed God.   *Spurgeon*

August 11

They that wait upon the Lord shall change their strength.   Isaiah 40:31 ERV

> Lord, what a change within us one
> short hour

Spent in Thy presence will prevail to
　　make!
What heavy burdens from our bosoms
　　take!
What parched grounds refresh as
　　with a shower!
We kneel—and all around us seems
　　to lower.
We rise—and all the distant and the
　　near
Stand forth in sunny outline, brave
　　and clear.
We kneel—how weak; we rise—how
　　full of power.

Why, therefore, should we do our-
　　selves this wrong
Or others—that we are not always
　　strong;
That we are ever overborne with
　　care;
That we should ever weak or heart-
　　less be,
Anxious or troubled, while with *us* is
　　prayer,
And joy and strength and courage
　　are with *Thee?*

Archbishop Trench

August 12

*As for thee, the Lord thy God hath not suffered
thee so to do.*   Deuteronomy 18:14

What a stepping-stone! We give thanks, often
with a tearful, doubtful voice, for our spiritual
mercies *positive;* but what an almost infinite

field there is for mercies *negative!* We cannot even imagine all that God has suffered us *not* to do, *not* to be.   *Frances Ridley Havergal*

August 13

Jesus went forth and saw a great multitude, and was moved with compassion toward them, and He healed their sick....And when He had sent the multitudes away, He went up into a mountain apart to pray; and when the evening was come He was there alone.
Matthew 14:14,23

Do we, like Him, combine the two great elements of human character? Are our *public* duties—the cares, and business, and engrossments of the world—finely tempered and hallowed by a *secret* walk with God? If the world were to follow us from its busy thoroughfares, would it trace us to our family altars and our closet devotions?

Action and meditation are the two great components of Christian life, and the perfection of the religious character is to find the two in unison and harmony.   *Macduff*

August 14

Leaving you an example, that ye should follow His steps.   1 Peter 2:21 ERV

I have long since ceased to pray, "Lord Jesus, have compassion on a lost world!" I remember the day and the hour when I seemed to hear the Lord rebuking me for making such a prayer. He seemed to say to me, "I have had compassion upon a lost world, and now it is for you to have compassion."   *A. J. Gordon*

August 15

Thou shalt have no other gods before me.
Exodus 20:3

If you find yourself beginning to love any pleasure better than your prayers, any book better than your Bible, any house better than God's, any table better than the Lord's, any person better than your Savior, any one better than your soul, a present indulgence better than the hope of heaven—take alarm!   *Guthrie*

August 16

Be ye followers of me, even as I also am of Christ.   1 Corinthians 11:1

When in the Mexican War the troops were wavering, a general rose in his stirrups and dashed into the enemy's line shouting, "Men, follow!" They, seeing his courage and disposition, dashed on after him and gained the victory.

What men want to rally them for God is an example to lead them. All your commands to others to advance amount to nothing so long as you stay behind. To effect them aright, you need to start for heaven yourself, looking back only to give the stirring cry of "Men, follow!"
T. DeWitt Talmage

August 17

Serving the Lord with all humility of mind.
Acts 20:19

There is a legend of an artist who long sought for a piece of sandalwood, out of which to carve a Madonna. He was about to give up in despair, leaving the vision of his life unrealized, when in a dream he was bidden to carve his Madonna from a block of oak wood which was destined for the fire. He obeyed, and produced a masterpiece from a log of common firewood.

Many of us lose great opportunities in life by waiting to find the sandalwood for our carvings, when they really lie hidden in the common logs that we burn.
Orison Swett Marden

August 18

My grace is sufficient for thee, for my strength is made perfect in weakness.
2 Corinthians 12:9

God's way of answering His people's prayers is not by removing the pressure, but by increasing their strength to bear it. The pressure is often the fence between the narrow way of life and the broad road to ruin; and if our Heavenly Father were to remove it, it might be at the sacrifice of heaven. Oh, if God had removed that thorny fence in answer, often to earnest prayers, how many of us would now be castaways! How the song of many a saint now in glory would be hushed! How many a harp would be unstrung! How many a place in the mansions of the redeemed would be unfilled! If God answered all the prayers we put up to heaven, we should need no other scourge. Blessed it is that we have One who is too loving to grant what we too often so rashly ask.   *F. Whitfield*

August 19

*Abide in me, and I in you. As the branch
cannot bear fruit of itself, except it abide in the
vine, no more can ye, except ye abide in me.*
John 15:4

From moment to moment, and from hour to
hour, the inner nature of man is to be continu-
ously sustained with the life of God. Only as I
am constantly receiving His fullness into my
emptiness am I really living in the true, full,
deep sense of the word that life of eternity,
which is my privilege now and will be my glory
hereafter. *W. Hay Aitken*

August 20

*By faith Noah . . . prepared an ark to the
saving of his house.* Hebrews 11:7

What a humble, what a modest sphere for the
exercise of faith! One would have said that the
purpose was quite disproportionate to the
work. The ark was a great undertaking, but
what was it undertaken for? To save his own
family. Is so narrow a sphere worthy to be the
object of faith? Is so commonplace a scene as
the life of the family circle fit to be a temple for
the service of God? . . . My soul, when thou hast
finished thy prayers and ended thy meditations,
do not say that thou hast left the house of God.
God's house shall to thee be everywhere, and
thine own house shall be a part of it. Thou shalt
feel that all the duties of this place are conse-
crated; that it is none other than the house of
God and one of the gates to heaven. Thou shalt

feel that every one of its duties is an act of high communion. Therefore be it thine to make thy house *His* house. Be it thine to consecrate each word and look and deed in the social life of home. Be it thine to build thine ark of refuge for the wants of common day; verily, thy labor of love shall be called an act of faith.
George Matheson

August 21

We are His workmanship, created in Christ Jesus unto good works which God hath before ordained that we should walk in them.
Ephesians 2:10

No man is born into the world whose work is not born with him. There is always work, and tools to work withal, for those who will.
J. R. Lowell

August 22

He . . . began to wash the disciples' feet.
John 13:5

We forget that Jesus Christ is the same today, when He is sitting on the throne, as He was yesterday, when He trod the pathway of our world. And in this forgetfulness how much we miss! What He was, that He is. What He said, that He says. The Gospels are simply specimens of the life that He is ever living; they are leaves torn out of the diary of His unchangeable Being. Today He is engaged in washing the feet of His disciples, soiled with their wilderness journeyings. Yes, that charming incident is having its fulfillment in thee, my friend, if only thou dost not refuse the lowly loving offices of Him whom we call Master and Lord, but who still girds Himself and comes forth to serve. And we *must* have this incessant cleansing if we would keep right. It is not enough to look back to a certain hour when we first knelt at the feet of the Son of God for pardon, and heard Him say, "Thy sins, which are many, are all forgiven." We need daily, hourly cleansing—from daily, hourly sin. *F. B. Meyer*

August 23

I am the Lord, I change not.   Malachi 3:6

Our hope is not hung upon such untwisted thread as "I imagine so" or "it is likely"; but the cable, the strong rope of our fastened anchor, is the oath and promise of Him who is eternal verity. Our salvation is fastened with God's own hand and Christ's own strength to the strong stake of God's unchanging nature.
William Rutherford

August 24

I will cause the shower to come down in his season; there shall be showers of blessing.
Ezekiel 34:26

What is thy *season* this morning? Is it the season of drought? Then that is the season for showers. Is it a season of great heaviness and black clouds? Then that is the season for showers. "As thy days, so shall thy strength be." "I will give thee *showers* of blessing." The word is in the plural. All kinds of blessings God will send. All God's blessings go together, like links in a golden chain. If He gives coverting grace, He will also give comforting grace. He will send "showers of blessings." Look up today, O parched plant, and open thy leaves and flowers for a heavenly watering. *Spurgeon*

August 25

Nevertheless, at thy word.   Luke 5:5

Oh, what a blessed formula for us! This path of mine is dark, mysterious, perplexing; *nevertheless, at Thy word* I will go forward. This trial of mine is cutting, sore for flesh and blood to bear. It is hard to breathe through a broken heart, "Thy will be done." But, *nevertheless, at Thy word* I will say, "Even so, Father!" This besetting habit, or infirmity, or sin of mine is difficult to crucify. It has become part of myself—a second nature; to be severed from it would be like the cutting off of a right hand, or the plucking out of a right eye; *nevertheless, at Thy word* I will lay aside every weight; this idol I will utterly abolish. This righteousness of mind it is hard to ignore; concerning all these virtues, and amiabilities, and natural graces, it is hard to believe that they dare not in any way be mixed up in the matter of my salvation, and that I am to receive all from first to last as the gift of God, through Jesus Christ my Lord. *Nevertheless, at Thy word* I will count all but loss for the excellency of His knowledge. *Macduff*

August 26

If we suffer, we shall also reign with Him.
2 Timothy 2:12

The photographer must have a negative in order to furnish you with a picture. Now the earthly cross is the negative from which the heavenly crown is to be made; the suffering and sorrow of the present time determine the glory, honor, and immortality of the life to come.
A. J. Gordon

August 27

The word of God, which liveth and abideth forever. 1 Peter 1:23

The Word abideth. The Jew hated it—but it lived on, while the veil was torn away from the shrine which the Shekinah had forsaken, and while Jerusalem itself was destroyed. The Greek derided it—but it has seen his philosophy effete and his Acropolis in ruins. The Romans threw it into the flames—but it rose from its ashes and swooped down upon the falling eagle. The reasoner cast it into the furnace, which his own negligence had heated "seven times hotter than its wont"—but it came out without the smell of fire. The formalist fastened serpents around it to poison it—but it shook them off and felt no harm. The infidel cast it overboard in a tempest of sophistry and sarcasm—but it rode gallantly upon the crest of the proud waters. And it is living still, yet heard in the loudest swelling of the storm. It has been speaking all the while—it is speaking now! *Punshon*

August 28

Let the peace of God rule in your hearts.
Colossians 3:15

Years ago one of our fleets was terribly shattered by a violent gale, but it was found that some of the ships were unaffected by its violence. They were in what mariners call "the eye of the storm." While all around was desolation, they were safe. So it is with him who has the peace of God in his heart.   *Pilkington*

August 29

Ye serve the Lord Christ.   Colossians 3:24

Our business as Christians is to serve the Lord in every business of life.   *Mark Guy Pearse*

August 30

Love not the world, neither the things that are in the world.   1 John 2:15

If you will go to the banks of a little stream, and watch the flies that come to bathe in it, you will notice that, while they plunge their *bodies* into the water, they keep their *wings* high out of the water; and, after swimming about a little while, they fly away with their wings unwet through the sunny air. Now that is the lesson for us. Here we are immersed in the cares and business of the world; but let us keep the wings of our soul, our faith and our love, out of the world, that, with these unclogged, we may be ready to take our flight to heaven.   *J. Inglis*

August 31

I would have you without carefulness.
1 Corinthians 7:32

Do not look forward to the changes and chances of this life in fear. Rather, look to them with full hope that, as they arise, God, whose you are, will deliver you out of them. He has kept you hitherto; do you but hold fast to His dear hand, and He will lead you safely through all things; and when you cannot stand, He will bear you in His arms. Do not look forward to what may happen tomorrow. The same everlasting Father who cares for you today will take care of you tomorrow, and every day. Either He will shield you from suffering, or He will give you unfailing strength to bear it. Be at peace then, and put aside all anxious thoughts and imaginations. *Francis de Sales*

September

September 1

Thus saith the Lord God, "I will yet for this be inquired of by the house of Israel, to do it for them." Ezekiel 36:37

Prayer is the forerunner of mercy. Turn to sacred history and you will find that scarcely ever did a great mercy come to this world unheralded by supplication. Prayer is always the preface to blessing. It goes before the blessing *as the blessing's shadow.* When the sunlight of God's mercies rises upon our necessities it casts the shadow of prayer far down upon the plain. Or, to use another illustration, when God piles up a hill of mercies He Himself shines behind them, and He casts on our spirits the shadow of prayer so that we may rest certain, if we are much in prayer, that our pleadings are the shadows of mercy. Prayer is thus connected with the blessing to show us the value of it. *Spurgeon*

September 2

Let us not be weary in well doing, for in due season we shall reap if we faint not. Galatians 6:9

The hours of this present life are the ages in embryo of the life to come. *A. J. Gordon*

September 3

My presence shall go with thee. Exodus 33:14

We should never leave our prayer closets in the morning without having concentrated our thoughts deeply and intensely on the fact of the actual presence of God there with us, encompassing us and filling the room as literally as it fills heaven itself. It may not lead to any distinct results at first, but as we make repeated efforts to realize the presence of God, it will become increasingly real to us. And as the habit grows upon us, when alone in a room, or when treading the grass of some natural woodland temple, or when pacing the stony street—in the silence of night, or amid the teeming crowds of daylight—we shall often find ourselves whispering the words, "Thou art near; Thou art here, O Lord." *F. B. Meyer*

September 4

To the Lord our God belong mercies and forgiveness. Daniel 9:9

As a spring lock closes itself, but cannot be unlocked without a key, so we ourselves may run into sin, but cannot return without the key of God's grace. *Cawdray*

September 5

It is high time to awake out of sleep. Romans 13:11

I have heard of a painter who loved to work by the morning light. He said that the colors were better understood by the light of the early day, and so he was wont to be in his studio waiting for the rising of the sun. Then every moment it grew lighter, and he found he could accomplish things which he could not reach if he waited till the day had advanced.

Is there not work waiting for us—work that no one else can do—work, too, that the Master has promised to help us perform? Shall He come and find that we still sleep? Or shall the Son of Righteousness, when He appears, find us waiting, as that painter waited, looking and longing for the first gleam of day? Surely those of us who thus wait on the Lord shall renew our strength, and, eagle-like, rise to greet the Sun.
Thomas Champness

September 6

The church of God, which He hath purchased with His own blood. Acts 20:28

Surely He may do what He will with His own. The price He has paid to make them His own is a sufficient guarantee that He will never make light of anything in which their welfare is at all concerned. We are precious to Him by the virtue of the blood which He has shed for us, and for Him to be found at any time wanting in solicitude for our happiness would be for Him to treat that blood of His as the sinners of this world treat it. The persuasion of Christ's love must be graven in our hearts so deeply that no semblance of indifference on His part will ever make the slightest impression upon us. This is the victory which overcometh the world.
George Bowen

September 7

The God of hope fill you with all joy and peace

in believing, that ye may abound in hope
through the power of the Holy Ghost.
Romans 15:13

In spiritual as in earthly things there is great
strength in hope, and therefore God's people
are carefully to cultivate that grace: a well-
grounded hope that, having been made new
creatures in Jesus Christ, we are His; that with
our names, though unknown to fame, written
in the Book of Life, we have grace in possession
and heaven in prospect; that after a few more
brief years, pure as the angels that sing before
the throne, we shall be brought with gladness
into the palace of the King, to be like Christ and
with Christ, seeing Him eye to eye and face to
face—such hopes are powerful springs of action.
Guthrie

September 8

He asked life of Thee, and Thou gavest it him,
even length of days for ever and ever.
Psalm 21:4

When poor men make requests of us we usually answer them as the echo does the voice—
the answer cuts off half the petition. We shall
seldom find among men Jael's courtesy, giving
milk to those that ask water, except it be as this
was, an entangling benefit, the better to intro-
duce a mischief. There are not many Naamans
among us, that, when you beg of them one talent, will force you to take two; but God's answer
to our prayers is like a magnifying glass, which
renders the request much greater in the answer
than it was in the prayer.   *Bishop Reynolds*

September 9

This beginning of miracles did Jesus.
John 2:11

It was out of the common thing that the precious thing was brought; and it is out of the common things of daily life, presented obediently to Jesus and laid at His feet, that He brings His own glorious gifts, so that our whole lives become one great sacrament.
W. Hay Aitken

September 10

In the daytime... He led them with a cloud, and all the night with a light of fire.
Psalm 78:14

My day is my prosperity; it is the time when the sun of fortune is bright above me, and therefore it is the time when I need a shade. If my sunshine were not checkered I would forget Thee, O my God.

But I have nights to meet as well as days. The night is my adversity; it is the time when the sun of fortune has gone down behind the hills, and I am left alone, and then it is, O my Father, that I need the light of Thy fire! My light of fire for the night is the vision of Calvary—the vision of Thy love in the Cross. I need the light of Thy fire "*all* the night." *George Matheson*

September 11

Now are we the sons of God, and it doth not yet appear what we shall be; but we know that

when He shall appear, we shall be like Him,
for we shall see Him as He is.   1 John 3:2

"Now are we the sons of God." That is the pier upon one side of the gulf. "It doth not yet appear what we shall be, but when He shall appear we shall be like Him." That is the pier on the other. How are the two to be connected? There is only one way by which the present sonship will blossom and fruit into the future perfect likeness: If we throw across the gulf, by God's help day by day, the bridge of growing likeness to Himself, and purity therefrom.
Alexander Maclaren

September 12

Behold, we go up to Jerusalem.   Matthew 20:18

Never had there been such a going up to Jerusalem as that which Jesus here proposes to His disciples. He goes up voluntarily. The act was not enforced by any external compulsion. Jerusalem might at this time have been avoided. Yet it was deliberately sought. It was a going up to a triumph to be reached through defeat, a coronation to be attained through ignominy and humiliation.

O believer, in your walk through the world today, be strengthened, be comforted, be inspired by the spectacle of the Captain of your salvation thus going up to Jerusalem! And remember, in all those apparently *downward* passages of life, where sorrow and even death lie before you, that all such descents, made or endured in the Spirit of Jesus, are really *upgoing* steps, leading you to the mount of God and the resurrection glory.   *J. B. Stratton*

September 13

These were the potters, and those that dwelt among plants and hedges; there they dwelt with the king for his work.   1 Chronicles 4:23

Anywhere and everywhere we may dwell "with the King for His work." We may be in a very unlikely or unfavorable place for this; it may be in a little country life, with little enough to be seen of the "goings" of the King around us; it may be among hedges of all sorts, hindrances in all directions; it may be with our hands full of all manner of pottery for our daily task. No matter! The King who placed us "there" will come and dwell there with us; the hedges are all right, or He would soon do away with them; and it does not follow that what seems to hinder our way may not be for its very protection; and as for the pottery, this is exactly what He has seen fit to put into our hands, and therefore it is, for the present, "His work."
Frances Ridley Havergal

September 14

I will instruct thee, and teach thee in the way which thou shalt go; I will guide thee with mine eye.   Psalm 32:8

When God does the directing, our life is useful and full of promise, whatever it is doing; and discipline has its perfecting work.
H. E. Cobb

September 15

The Son of man came not to be ministered

*unto, but to minister, and to give His life a
ransom for many.* Matthew 20:28

We are so to surrender ourselves to Christ
that this great purpose of His coming shall
claim and possess the whole life. We are to live,
like God, to bless others. This is His will, His
purpose concerning us. This is what His power
waits to do for us. And this too is the claim of
His great love upon us.

Do not sigh a poor assent to the truth of it,
and then pass by neglectfully on the other side.
Do not think about it and pray about it without
even a passing hope that the prayer will be
answered. Do not gather yourself up in great
resolutions to be good and useful. Kneel in
sight of the Crucified. In the cross of Christ
spell out His great purpose and yearning love to
men. Let the heart feel all the might of the
appeal that comes to us from those torn hands
and feet and bleeding brow, from all the dread-
ful shame and agony of our dear Lord. And,
bought and bound by all this, surrender yourself to Him for His great purpose. Take Him as
your strength for this life-work.
Mark Guy Pearse

September 16

Jesus...went about doing good. Acts 10:38

The finest of all fine arts is the art of doing
good; and yet it is the least cultivated.
T. DeWitt Talmage

September 17

The angel of the Lord said unto her [Hagar],

"Return to thy mistress, and submit thyself under her hands." Genesis 16:9

SUBMISSION is a great Christian law, but we find it early in Genesis, early in the history of mankind, and angel-given. *Selected*

September 18

Then spoke Solomon, "... I have surely built thee an house to dwell in." 1 Kings 8:12,13

Solomon, the prince of peace, alone could build the temple. If we would be soulwinners and build up the church, which is God's temple, let us note this: Not by discussion nor by argument, but by lifting up Christ, shall we draw men unto Him. *J. Hudson Taylor*

September 19

I have chosen thee in the furnace of affliction. Isaiah 48:10

Does not the word come like a soft shower, assuaging the fury of the flame? Yea, is it not an asbestos armor, against which the heat hath no power? Let affliction come—God has chosen me. Poverty, thou mayest stride in at my door—but God is in the house already, and He has chosen me. Sickness, thou mayest intrude, but I have a balsam ready—God has chosen me. Whatever befalls me in this vale of tears I know that He has chosen me. Fear not, Christian; Jesus is with thee. In all thy fiery trials His presence is both thy comfort and safety. He will never leave one whom He has chosen for His own. "Fear not, for I am with thee" is His sure word of promise to His chosen ones in the furnace of affliction.   *Spurgeon*

September 20

Base things of the world and things which are despised hath God chosen.   1 Corinthians 1:28

In some of the great halls of Europe may be seen pictures not painted with the brush, but mosaics, which are made up of small pieces of stone, glass, or other material. The artist takes these little pieces, and, polishing and arranging them, he forms them into the grand and beautiful picture. Each individual part of the picture may be a little worthless piece of glass or marble or shell; but, with each in its place, the whole constitutes the masterpiece of art.

So I think it will be with humanity in the hands of the great Artist. God is picking up the little worthless pieces of stone and brass that might be trodden underfoot unnoticed, and is making of them His great masterpiece.
Bishop Simpson

September 21

Serve the Lord with gladness; come before His presence with singing.   Psalm 100:2

God wants our life to be a song. He has written the music for us in His Word and in the duties that come to us in our places and relations in life. The things we ought to do are the notes set upon the staff. To make our life beautiful music we must be obedient and submissive.

Any disobedience is the singing of a false note, and yields discord.   *J. R. Miller*

September 22

When thou prayest, enter into thy closet, and when thou hast shut thy door, pray to thy Father, who is in secret.   Matthew 6:6

This is faith's stronghold; here she weapons herself for the daily conflict. Silence in that closet of prayer bespeaks death throughout all the house. When that door is permitted to rust on its hinges, and that chamber is deserted, then the heart-house is soon retaken by Satan, and evil spirits come in and dwell there.
Theodore Cuyler

September 23

Be ye holy, for I am holy.   1 Peter 1:16

The highway of holiness is along the commonest road of life—along your very way. In wind and rain, no matter how it beats, it is only going hand in hand with Him.
Mark Guy Pearse

September 24

And the Lord said, "Shall I hide from Abraham that thing which I do?"
Genesis 18:17

Abraham, in communion with God, knew long before Lot, in Sodom, of the destruction of that city. Oh, for more communion!   *Selected*

September 25

The life which I now live in the flesh.
Galatians 2:20

I expect to pass through this world but once; therefore, if there be any kindness I can show or any good thing I can do to any fellow human being, let me do it *now;* let me not defer or neglect it, for I shall not pass this way again.
Marcus Aurelius

September 26

So teach us to number our days that we may apply our hearts unto wisdom.   Psalm 90:12

Every day is a little life, and our whole life is but a day repeated. Thus old Jacob numbers his life by days, and Moses desires to be taught this point of holy arithmetic—to number not his years, but his days. Those therefore that dare lose a day are dangerously prodigal; those that dare misspend it, desperate.   *Bishop Hall*

September 27

Christ in you the hope of glory.
Colossians 1:27

Religion is not the simple fire escape that you build in anticipation of a possible danger, upon the outside of your dwelling, and leave there until danger comes. You go to it some morning when a fire breaks out in your house, and the poor old thing that you built up there, and thought that you could use someday, is so rusty and broken, and the weather has so beaten upon it and the sun so turned its hinges, that it will not work. That is the condition of a man who has built himself what seems a creed of faith, a trust in God in anticipation of the day when danger is to overtake him, and has said to himself, "I am safe, for I will take refuge in it then." But religion is the house in which we live, it is the table at which we sit, it is the fireside at which we draw near, the room that arches its graceful and familiar presence over us; it is the bed on which we lie and think of the past, and anticipate the future, and gather our refreshment. *Phillips Brooks*

September 28

Wait for the promise of the Father. Acts 1:4

Tarry at a promise till God meets you there. He always returns by way of His promises.
Selected

September 29

This is the victory that overcometh the world, even our faith. 1 John 5:4

The world conquers me when it succeeds in hindering me from seeing, loving, holding communion with, and serving my Father God. I conquer it when I lay my hand upon it and force it to help me to get nearer Him, to get more like Him, to think oftener of Him, to do His will more gladly and more constantly. The one victory over the world is to bend it to serve me in the highest things—the attainment of a clearer vision of the divine nature, the attainment of a deeper love to God Himself, and a more glad consecration and service to Him. That is the victory—when you can make the world a ladder to lift you to God. When the world comes between you and God as an obscuring screen, it has conquered you. When the world comes between you and God as a transparent medium, you have conquered it. To win victory is to get it beneath your feet and stand upon it, and reach up thereby to God. *Alexander Maclaren*

September 30

He shall give His angels charge over thee, to keep thee in all thy ways. Psalm 91:11

Count no duty too little, no round of life too small, no work too low, if it come in thy way, since God thinks so much of it as to send His angels to guard thee in it. *Mark Guy Pearse*

October

October 1

At Jesus' feet.   Luke 10:39

At Jesus' feet—that is our place of privilege and of blessing, and here it is that we are to be educated and fitted for the practical duties of life. Here we are to renew our strength while we wait on Him, and to learn how to mount on wings as eagles; and here we are to become possessed of that true knowledge which is power. Here we are to learn how real work is to be done, and to be armed with the true motive power to do it. Here we are to find solace amidst both the trials of work—and they are not few— and the trials of life in general; and here we are to anticipate something of the blessedness of heaven amidst the days of earth; for to sit at His feet is indeed to be in heavenly places, and to gaze upon His glory is to do what we shall never tire of doing yonder.   *W. Hay Aitken*

October 2

God is love; and he that dwelleth in love dwelleth in God, and God in him.
1 John 4:16

God is love; and it is good, as it is true, to think that every sun-ray that touches the earth has the sun at the other end of it; so every bit of love upon God's earth has God at the other end of it.
Mark Guy Pearse

October 3

They took knowledge of them that they had been with Jesus.   Acts 4:13

A Christian should be a striking likeness of Jesus Christ. You have read lives of Christ, beautifully and eloquently written, but the best life of Christ is His living biography, written out in the words and actions of His people. If we were what we profess to be, and what we should be, we would be pictures of Christ; yea, such striking likenesses of Him that the world would not have to hold us up by the hour together, and say, "Well, it seems somewhat of a likeness"; but they would, when they once beheld us, exclaim, "He has been with Jesus; he has been taught of Him; he is like Him; he has caught the very idea of the holy Man of Nazareth, and he works it out in his life and everyday actions."   *Spurgeon*

October 4

Be not afraid, only believe.   Mark 5:36

Be not downcast if difficulties and trials surround you in your heavenly life. They may be purposely placed there by God to train and discipline you for higher developments of faith. If He calls you to "toiling in rowing," it may be to make you the hardier seaman, to lead you to lift up the hands which hang down, and the feeble knees, and above all to drive you to a holier trust in Him who has the vessel and its destinies in His hand, and who, amid gathering clouds and darkened horizon and crested billows, is ever uttering the mild rebuke to our misgivings, "Said I not unto thee, if thou wouldest believe, thou shouldst see the glory of God?"
Macduff

October 5

Happy is the man whom God correcteth.
Job 5:17

Happy, because the correction is designed to bring him into paths of blessedness and peace.

Happy, because there is no unnecessary severity in it.

Happy, because the chastisement is not so much against us as against our most cruel enemies—our sins.

Happy, because we have abundant words of consolation.

Happy, because whom the Lord loveth He chasteneth.

Happy, because our light affliction is but for a moment.   *George Bowen*

October 6

When they saw the star they rejoiced with exceeding great joy.   Matthew 2:10

We who look for Jesus ought to be joyful; it is no credit to our Lord when we look as though we were seeking His grave. The dull looks of Christ's followers have injured Him in the sight of the world. Let us then smile as we go, for we have the star if we will look up and put ourselves in the right path.   *Thomas Champness*

October 7

When I sit in darkness the Lord shall be a light unto me.   Micah 7:8

If you are willing to choose the seeming darkness of faith instead of the illumination of reason, wonderful light will break out upon you from the Word of God.   *A. J. Gordon*

October 8

I [Daniel] was left alone, and saw this great vision.   Daniel 10:8

Solitude is the antechamber of God; only one step more and you can be in His immediate presence.   *Landor*

October 9

Come and dine.   John 21:12

This morning the voice of the Beloved of our soul is heard giving us His invitation.

"Children," He asks, "have ye any meat?"

We answer, "No; of ourselves we have nothing but hunger and starvation. O God, we cannot feed ourselves!"

Then it is that His own sweet voice replies, "Come and dine!"   *W. Hay Aitken*

October 10

O Lord God, Thou knowest! Ezekiel 37:3

Here is the response of faith. "Thou knowest!"—what a pillow for the heart to repose upon! "Thou knowest!"—what few but comprehensive words to sum up and express the heart's difficulties and perplexities and trials. "Thou knowest!"—what an inexpressibly sweet resting-place in the midst of life's tumultuous heavings; in the midst of a sea that knows no calm; in the midst of a scene in which tossings to and fro are the hourly history! What an answer they contain for every heart that can find no words to express its big emotions; for a heart whose sorrows are too deep for language to find its way to God! Oh, that they were ever uppermost in the soul as the response to every difficulty in our path! They are God's answer to everything we cannot fathom; God's answer for our hearts to rest upon and our lips to utter when every way is hedged up so that we cannot pass. "O Lord God, thou knowest!" Rest here, believer. Lean thy soul on these words. Repose calmly on the bosom of thy God, and carry them with thee into every scene of life. "O Lord God, thou knowest."   *F. Whitfield*

October 11

Behold, a ladder set up on the earth, and the top of it reached to heaven.   Genesis 28:12

Think of that mystic ladder which descends from the throne of God to the spot, however lowly, where you may be. It may be a moorland waste, a humble cottage, a ship's cabin, a settler's hut, a bed of pain; but Jesus Christ finds you out, and comes just where you are. The one pole of this ladder is the gold of His deity; the other is the silver of His manhood; the rungs are the series of events from the cradle of Bethlehem to the right hand of power, where He sits. That ladder sways beneath a weight of blessing for you. Oh, that you would send away your burdens of sin, and care, and fear, by the

hands of the ascending angels of prayer and faith, and receive into your heart the trooping angels of peace, and joy, and love, and glory!
F. B. Meyer

October 12

Surely God is in this place, and I knew it not.
Genesis 28:16

The Parish priest, of austerity,
Climbed up in the high church steeple
To be nearer God, that he might hand
His word down to the people.
And in the sermon script he daily wrote
What he thought was sent from heaven;
And he dropped it down on the people's
   heads
Two times one day in seven.
In his age God said, "Come down and die."
And he cried out from the steeple:
"Where art Thou, Lord?" and the Lord
   replied:
"Down here among my people."   *Selected*

October 13

Now therefore, hearken, O Israel, unto the statutes and unto the judgments which I teach you, for to do them, that ye may live, and go in and possess the land which the Lord God of your fathers giveth you. Deuteronomy 4:1

"Hearken" and "do" that ye may "live" and "possess." This is a universal and abiding principle. It was true for Israel, and it is true for us.

The pathway of life and the true secret of possession is simple obedience to the holy commandments of God. We see this all through the inspired volume, from cover to cover. God has given us His Word, not to speculate upon it or discuss it, but that we may obey it. And it is as we, through grace, yield a hearty and happy obedience to our Father's statutes and judgments that we tread the bright pathway of life, and enter into the reality of all that God has treasured up for us in Christ.   *C. H. Mackintosh*

October 14

I live; yet not I, but Christ liveth in me; and the life which I now live in the flesh I live by the faith of the Son of God, who loved me and gave Himself for me. Galatians 2:20

The man who lives in God knows no life except the life of God.   *Phillips Brooks*

October 15

Let us who are of the day be sober, putting on the breastplate of faith and love, and for a helmet the hope of salvation.
1 Thessalonians 5:8

Faith, love, hope—these three form the defensive armor that guards the soul; and these three make self-control possible. Like a diver in his suit who is let down to the bottom of the wild, far-weltering ocean, a man whose heart is girded by faith and charity, and whose head is covered with the helmet of hope, may be dropped down into the wildest sea of temptation and of worldliness, and yet will walk dry and unharmed through the midst of its depths, and breathe air that comes from a world above the restless surges. *Faith* will bring you into communication with all the power of God. *Love* will lead you into a region where all the temptations round you will be touched as by Ithuriel's spear, and will show their own foulness. And *hope* will turn away your eyes from looking at the tempting splendor around, and fix them upon the glories that are above. And so the reins will come into your hands in an altogether new manner, and you will be able to be king over your own nature in a fashion that you did not dream of before, if only you will trust in Christ and love Him, and fix your desires on the things above. Then you will be able to govern yourself, when you let Christ govern you.

Alexander Maclaren

October 16

The word of our God shall stand forever.
Isaiah 40:8

The Word of God is the water of life; the more ye pour it forth, the fresher it runneth. It is the fire of God's glory; the more ye blow it, the clearer it burneth. It is the corn of the Lord's field; the better ye grind it, the more it yieldeth. It is the bread of heaven; the more it is broken and given forth, the more it remaineth. It is the sword of the Spirit; the more it is scoured, the brighter it shineth. *Bishop Jewel*

October 17

I spoke unto thee in thy prosperity.
Jeremiah 22:21

We shade our eyes with the hand to shut out
the glare of the strong daylight when we want
to see far away. God thus puts, as it were, His
hand upon our brows, and tempers the glow of
prosperity, that we may take in the wider phases
of His goodness. It is a common experience
that, looking out from the gloom of some personal affliction, men have seen for the first time
beyond the earth plane, and caught glimpses of
the Beulah Land. Let us not shrink from the
Hand which we know is heavy only with blessing. *Ludlow*

October 18

*Surely He shall deliver thee from the snare of
the fowler.* Psalm 90:3

He shall deliver thee from the snare of the fowler.
That is, from the little things, the hidden traps
and nets that are set for us. Great sins frighten
where little snares entangle. It is easier to
escape the huntsman's arrow than the crafty
lure.

And where are they not set? Riches and poverty, sickness and strength, prosperity and
adversity, friendship and loneliness, the work
and the want of it—each has its snare, wherein
not only are the unwary caught, but the wise
and the watchful sometimes fall a prey. Little
things, mere threads, hardly worth guarding
against—yet they are strong enough to hold us

and hinder us, and may be the beginning of our destruction.   *Mark Guy Pearse*

October 19

The Lord set a mark upon Cain.   Genesis 4:15

We speak of the mark of Cain as if it were the mark of a curse. In reality it was the mark of God's mercy, a defense against his enemies. *D. J. Burrell*

October 20

*Who is among you that feareth the Lord...
that walketh in darkness and hath no light?
Let him trust in the name of the Lord, and
stay upon his God.*   Isaiah 1:10

"In fierce storms," said an old seaman, "we can do but one thing, there is only one way: We must put the ship in a certain position and keep her there."

This, Christian, is what you must do. Sometimes, like Paul, you can see neither sun nor stars, and no small tempest lies on you; and then you can do but one thing; there is only one way. Reason cannot help you. Past experiences give you no light. Even prayer fetches no consolation. Only a single course is left: You must put your soul in one position and keep it there. You must stay upon the Lord; and, come what may—winds, waves, cross seas, thunder, lightning, frowning rocks, roaring breakers—no matter what, you must lash yourself to the helm, and hold fast your confidence in God's faithfulness, His covenant engagement, His everlasting love in Christ Jesus.   *Richard Fuller*

October 21

Be thou faithful unto death, and I will give thee a crown of life.   Revelation 2:10

There is a heaven at the end of every faithful Christian's journey.   *Cuyler*

October 22

Flee into Egypt.   Matthew 2:13

Why? Because there is a cruel king who will seek the young child's life.

Is Christ born in thee? Is thy life like that manger—precious as a casket, because of what it holds? Then have a care; for, craftier and more unscrupulous than Herod, the destroyer of souls will seek to destroy thee.

There is a day coming when they shall say, "They are dead which sought the young child's life." Grace shall survive the foe, and we shall yet return to enjoy the comforts of life, with no Herod to threaten us. After all, it is sin which is short-lived, for goodness shall flourish when the evil one is chained up forever.
Thomas Champness

October 23

As my lord the king hath said, so will thy servant do.   1 Kings 2:38

There is something infinitely better than doing a great thing for God, and the infinitely better thing is to be where God wants us to be, to do what God wants us to do, and to have no will apart from His.   *G. Campbell Morgan*

October 24

Let your light so shine before men that they may see your good works and glorify your Father who is in heaven.   Matthew 5:16

They say the world has an eagle eye for anything inconsistent, an eye sharp to discover the vagaries and inconsistencies in the defaulty and the unworthy. It has an eagle eye; but the eagle winks before the sun, and the burning iris of its eye shrinks abashed before the unsullied purity of noon. Let your light so shine before men that others, awed and charmed by the consistency of your godly life, may come to inquire, and to say you have been with Jesus.   *Punshon*

October 25

The eleven disciples went . . . into a mountain where Jesus had appointed them . . . . Jesus came and spoke unto them, saying, ". . . Go ye and teach all nations."   Matthew 28:16,18,19

The considerable actions in the world have usually very small beginnings. Of a few letters, how many thousand words are made! Of ten figures, how many thousand numbers! A point is the beginning of all geometry. A little stone flung into a pond makes a little circle, then a greater, till it enlarges itself to both the sides. So from small beginnings God doth cause an efflux through the whole word.   *Charnock*

October 26

Behold, I bring you good tidings of great joy, which shall be to all people.   Luke 2:10

It is true that these good tidings of great joy were to be "for all people," but not *first*. The message falls on our own ears, and is first for our own souls.

Oh, ponder this well! Take all God's truths home *first* to thine own heart. Ask in earnest prayer that the Spirit may write them with the pen of heaven on thine own conscience. Then wilt thou be a vessel fitted for the Master's use, and carry His message with spiritual power to the souls of others.   *F. Whitfield*

October 27

Whom the Lord loveth He chasteneth.
Hebrews 12:6

Earthly prosperity is no sign of the special love of heaven; nor are sorrow and care any mark of God's disfavor, but the reverse. God's love is robust, and true, and eager—not for our comfort, but for our lasting blessedness. It is bent on achieving this, and it is strong enough to bear misrepresentation and rebuke in its attempts to attune our spirits to higher music. It therefore comes instructing us. Let us enter ourselves as pupils in the school of God's love. Let us lay aside our own notions of the course of study; let us submit ourselves to be led and taught; let us be prepared for any lessons that may be given from the blackboard of sorrow; let us be so assured of the inexhaustible tenacity of His love as to dare to trust Him though He slay us. And let us look forward to that august moment when He will give us a reason for all life's discipline, with a smile that shall thrill our souls with ecstasy, and constrain sorrow and sighing to flee away forever.   *F. B. Meyer*

October 28

Whatsoever ye shall ask the Father in my name, He will give it you.   John 16:23

Prayer must be based upon promise, but, thank God, His promises are always broader than our prayers! No fear of building inverted pyramids here, for Jesus Christ is the foundation.   *Frances Ridley Havergal*

October 29

He riseth from supper and laid aside His garments, and took a towel and girded Himself. After that He poureth water into a basin, and began to wash the disciples' feet, and to wipe them with the towel wherewith He was girded.   John 13:4,5

Acts are common and mean because they are ordinarily expressive of the common and mean thoughts of men. Let us not accuse the acts that make up our daily life of meanness, but our ignoble souls that reveal themselves so unworthily through those acts. The same act may successively mount up through every intermediate stage from the depth of unworthiness to a transcendent height of excellence, according to the soul that is manifested by it. One of the glorious ends of our Lord's incarnation was that He might propitiate us with the details of life, so that we should not disdain these as insignificant, but rather disdain ourselves for our inability to make these details interpreters of a noble nature. Oh, let us then look with affectionateness and gratitude upon the daily details of life, seeing the sanctifying imprint of the hand of Jesus upon them all!   *George Bowen*

October 30

He placed ... cherubims and a flaming sword ... to keep the way of the tree of life.
Genesis 3:24

Blessed are they that do His commandments, that they may have right to the tree of life.
Revelation 22:14

How remarkable and how beautiful it is that the last page of the Revelation should come bending round to touch the first page of Genesis. The history of man began with angels with frowning faces and flaming swords barring the way to the Tree of Life. It ends with the guard of cherubim withdrawn; or rather, perhaps, sheathing their swords and becoming guides to the no longer forbidden fruit, instead of being its guards. That is the Bible's grand symbolical way of saying that all between—the sin, the misery, the death—is a parenthesis. God's purpose is not going to be thwarted. The end of His majestic march through history is to be men's access to the Tree of Life, from which, for the dreary ages—that are but as a moment in the great eternities—they were barred out by their sin. *Alexander Maclaren*

October 31

That the God of our Lord Jesus Christ, the Father of glory, may give unto you the spirit of wisdom and revelation in the knowledge of Him, the eyes of your understanding being enlightened. Ephesians 1:17,18

We were coming down a mountain in Switzerland one evening when a black thunderstorm blotted out the day, and all things were suddenly plunged into darkness. We could only dimly see the narrow, dusty footpaths, and the gloomy sides that were swallowed up in deeper gloom. What then of the majesty all about us—heights, and depths, and wonders? All was darkness. Then came the lightning—not flashes, but the blazing of the whole sky, incessant and on every side. What recesses of glory we gazed into! What marvels of splendor shone out of the darkness!

Think how with us, in us, is One who comes to make the common, dusty ways of life resplendent, illuminating our dull thoughts by the light of the glory of God; clearing the vision of the soul, and then revealing the greatness of the salvation that is ours in Christ.

Mark Guy Pearse

November

November 1

Jesus was left alone, and the woman standing in the midst. John 8:9

Alone with Jesus! What a sweet and holy spot! What a blessed refuge to which the soul may betake itself from the charges of Satan, the accusations of the world, and the sorrows of life! Sweet spot for the heart to unfold itself, to tell its hidden tale in the ear of infinite love, tenderness, and compassion!

Alone with Jesus! How different a front would Christianity present to the world if the Lord's people were oftener there! What humility, and gentleness, and love, would characterize all their dealings! What holiness stamped on the very brow, that all might read! What few judgments passed on others, how many more on ourselves! What calmness and resignation and joyful submission to all the Lord's dealings!

Be much "alone with Jesus." Then will the passage to glory be one of sunshine, whether it be through the portals of the grave or through the clouds of heaven. *F. Whitfield*

November 2

Thou wilt show me the path of life: in Thy presence is fullness of joy; at Thy right hand there are pleasures for evermore. Psalm 16:11

The man who walks along the path of life lives in the presence of the joy-giving God. Just insofar as he is true to that path of life, and wanders neither to the right hand nor to the left, his joy becomes deeper, and he becomes partaker of that very fullness of joy in which God Himself lives and moves and has His being. And while such is his experience in the midst of all the trials of life, he has also the privilege of looking forward to grander things yet in store for him, when that higher world shall be reached and the shadows of time have passed away forever. "At Thy right hand," exclaims the psalmist, "there are pleasures for evermore."

W. Hay Aitken

November 3

Be clothed with humility.   1 Peter 5:5

Is it not one of the difficulties of church work that we have more officers than men? We need more of the rank and file, who are willing to march anywhere and to do the lowliest of tasks. We shall succeed in doing greater things when all of us are willing to be subject. It is the bayonet rather than the gold lace which is wanted when the enemy is to be subdued.

Thomas Champness

November 4

Jacob lifted up his eyes, and looked and behold, Esau came, and with him four hundred men.
Genesis 33:1

Do not lift up your eyes and look for Esau. Those who look for troubles will not be long without finding trouble to look at. Lift them higher—to Him from whom our help cometh. Then you will be able to meet your troubles with an unperturbed spirit. Those who have seen the face of God need not fear the face of man that shall die. To have power with God is to have power over all the evils that threaten us. *F. B. Meyer*

November 5

Let us cleanse ourselves from all filthiness of the flesh and spirit, perfecting holiness in the fear of God. 2 Corinthians 7:1

The Tree of Life, according to some of the old rabbinical legends, lifted its branches, by an indwelling motion, high above impure hands that were stretched to touch them; and until our hands are cleansed through faith in Jesus Christ, its richest fruit hangs unreachable, golden above our heads. The fullness of the life of heaven is only granted to those who, drawing near Jesus Christ by faith on earth, have thereby cleansed themselves from all filthiness of the flesh and spirit. *Alexander Maclaren*

November 6

The pillar of the cloud went from before their face, and stood behind them. Exodus 14:19

It is not always guidance that we most need. Many of our dangers come upon us from behind. They are stealthy, insidious, assaulting us when we are unaware of their nearness. The tempter is cunning and shrewd. He does not meet us full front. It is a comfort to know that Christ comes behind us when it is there we need the protection. *J. R. Miller*

November 7

*Iniquities prevail against me; as for our
transgressions, Thou shalt purge them away.*
Psalm 65:3

There is much earnest religion that lives in
the dreary compass of these first four words,
"Iniquities prevail against me," and never gets
a glimpse beyond it. But do not put a full stop
there. Fetch in One who can help. "As for our
transgressions, THOU shalt purge them away."
The moment we bring the Lord in, that moment
defeat is turned to triumphant deliverance!

Write that up in golden letters—THOU! And
do not find in this word only a trembling hope
or a wondering wish. Listen to its full assurance—
THOU SHALT!

There is but one result that can warrant the
agony of Calvary; there is but one result that
can satisfy either our blessed Savior or ourselves; and that is our being conquerors over
sin.   *Mark Guy Pearse*

November 8

Speaking the truth in love.   Ephesians 4:15

The best way of eradicating error is to pub-
lish and practice truth.   *W. Arnot*

November 9

So he arose, and went to Zarephath.
1 Kings 17:10

Let it be equally said of you to whatever duty
the Lord may call you away, "He arose and

went." Be the way ever so laborious or dangerous, still arise, like Elijah, and go. Go cheerfully, in faith, keeping your heart quietly dependent on the Lord, and in the end you will surely behold and sing of His goodness. Though tossed on a sea of troubles, you may anchor on the firm foundation of God, which standeth sure. You have for your security His exceeding great and precious promises, and may say with the psalmist, "Why art thou cast down, O my soul? And why art thou disquieted within me? Hope thou in God, for I shall yet praise Him, who is the health of my countenance and my God."   *F. W. Krummacher*

November 10

A daily rate for every day.   2 Kings 25:30.

The acts of breathing which I performed yesterday will not keep me alive today; I must continue to breathe afresh every moment, or physical life ceases. In like manner yesterday's grace and spiritual strength must be renewed, and the Holy Spirit must continue to breathe on my soul from moment to moment in order to my enjoying the consolations, and to my working the works of God.   *Toplady*

November 11

When the vessel that he made of the clay was marred in the hand of the potter, he made it again another vessel, as seemed good to the potter to make it.   Jeremiah 18:4 ERV

God's fairest, highest place of service in the land that lies beyond will be filled by the men and women who have been broken upon the wheel on the earth.   *G. Campbell Morgan*

November 12

Examine yourselves.   2 Corinthians 13:5

If your state be good, searching into it will give you that comfort of it. If your state be bad, searching into it cannot make it worse; nay, it is the only way to make it better, for conversion begins with conviction.   *Bishop Hopkins*

November 13

Choose you this day whom ye will serve.
Joshua 24:15

CHOICE AND SERVICE—these were demanded of the Israelites; these are demanded of you, these only. Choice and service—in these are the whole of life. *Mark Hopkins*

November 14

Lord, thou has been our dwelling place in all generations.   Psalm 90:1

You cannot detain the eagle in the forest. You may gather around him a chorus of the choicest birds; you may give him a perch on the goodliest pine; you may charge winged messengers to bring him the choicest dainties; but he will spurn them all. Spreading his lordly wings, and with his eye on the Alpine cliff, he will soar away to his own ancestral halls amid the munitions of rocks and the wild music of tempest and waterfall.

The soul of man, in its eagle soarings, will

rest with nothing short of the Rock of Ages. Its ancestral halls are the halls of heaven. Its munitions of rocks are the attributes of God. The sweep of its majestic flight is Eternity! "Lord, THOU hast been our dwelling place in all generations!" *Macduff*

November 15

He hath said.   Hebrews 13:5

If we can only grasp these words of faith, we have an all-conquering weapon in our hand. What doubt is there that will not be slain by this two-edged sword? What fear is there which shall not fall smitten with a deadly wound before this arrow from the bow of God's covenant? "He hath said!" Whether for delight in our quietude or for strength in our conflict, "He hath said!" must be our daily resort.

Since "He hath said" is the source of all wisdom and the fountain of all comfort, let it dwell in you richly as "a well of water, springing up unto everlasting life." So shall you grow healthy, strong, and happy in the divine life.   *Spurgeon*

November 16

Not I, but Christ liveth in me.
Galatians 2:20

The wonder of the life in Jesus is this—and you will find it so, and you *have* found it so, if you have ever taken your New Testament and tried to make it the rule of your daily life—that there is not a single action that you are called upon to do of which you need be in any serious

doubt as to what Jesus Christ would have you do under those circumstances and with the material upon which you are called to act. The soul that takes in Jesus' word, the soul that through the words of Jesus enters into the very person of Jesus, the soul that knows Him as its daily presence and its daily law—it never hesitates.
Phillips Brooks

November 17

Who is my neighbor? Luke 10:29

"Who is thy neighbor?" It is the sufferer—wherever, whoever, whatsoever he be. Wherever thou hearest the cry of distress, wherever thou seest anyone brought across thy path by the chances and changes of life (that is, by the providence of God), whom it is in thy power to help—he, stranger or enemy though he be—*he* is thy neighbor.   *A. P. Stanley*

November 18

He which stablisheth us . . . in Christ, and hath anointed us, is God; who hath also sealed us and given the earnest of the Spirit in our hearts. 2 Corinthians 1:21,22

When a Christian is sealed by the Holy Ghost, sealed as the property of his Master, there will be no need to ask, "Whose image and superscription is this?" upon the sealed one. The King's, of course. Anyone can see the image.

Of what use is a seal if it cannot be seen?

Is the King's image visibly and permanently stamped upon us? It is on every Spirit-filled, sealed believer.   *John McNeil*

November 19

They shall rejoice, and shall see the plummet in the hand of Zerubbabel.   Zechariah 4:10

It is joy to the Christian to know that the plummet is now in the hands of our great Zerubbabel, and that when He comes forth, the world's misrule shall be over. The false standards and false estimates of men shall be swept away. The standards of expediency, of "conscience," of "every man thinking as he likes, if he is only *sincere*"—these and all similar refuges of lies shall be like a spider's web. The measure of all things will be Christ, and Christ the Measurer of all things.

How everything will be reversed! What a turning upside down of all that now exists!

Blessed day, and longed for—the world's great jubilee, the earth's long-looked-for Sabbath, groaning creation's joy, and nature's calm repose! Who would not cry, "Come, Lord Jesus, and end this troubled dream! Shatter the shadows of the long, dark night of sin and sorrow, sighing and tears, despair and death!"
F. Whitfield

November 20

In the world ye shall have tribulation; but be of good cheer: I have overcome the world.
John 16:33

Tribulation is God's threshing—not to destroy us, but to get what is good, heavenly, and spiritual in us separated from what is wrong, earthly, and fleshly. Nothing less than blows of pain will do this. The evil clings so to the good, the golden wheat of goodness in us is so wrapped up in the strong chaff of the old life, that only the heavy flail of suffering can produce the separation.   *J. R. Miller*

November 21

I . . . heard behind me a great voice, as of a trumpet, saying, ". . . Write."
Revelation 1:10,11

It is very sweet to note that a voice from heaven said to John, "Write." Does not that voice come to us? Are there not those who would taste the joys of heaven if we wrote them words of forgiveness and affection? Are there not others who would dry their tears if we would remind them of past joys, when we were poor as they are now? Could not some who read these words place inside an envelope something bearing their signature which would make a widow's heart dance for joy?

What is our pen doing? Is it adding joy to other men's lives? If so, then angels may tune their harps when we sit at our desk. They are sent to minister to the heirs of salvation, and would be glad to look upon our pen as writing music for them to sing, because what we write makes their client's joy to be full.
Thomas Champness

November 22

Whom the Lord loveth He chasteneth.
Hebrews 12:6

We should ever bear in mind that the discipline of our heavenly Father's hand is to be interpreted in the light of our Father's countenance; and the deep mysteries of His moral government to be contemplated through the medium of His tender love. *Selected*

November 23

Faithful is He that calleth you, who also will do it. 1 Thessalonians 5:24

Earthly faithfulness is possible only by the reception of heavenly gifts. As surely as every leaf that grows is mainly water that the plant has gotten from the clouds, and carbon that it has gotten out of the atmosphere, so surely will all our good be mainly drawn from heaven and heaven's gifts. As certainly as every lump of coal that you put upon your fire contains in itself sunbeams that have been locked up for all these millennia that have passed since it waved green in the forest, so certainly does every good deed embody in itself gifts from above. No man is pure except by impartation; every good thing and every perfect thing cometh from the Father of lights. *Alexander Maclaren*

November 24

Singing with grace in your hearts to the Lord. Colossians 3:16

Remember that your life is to be a singing life. This world is God's grand cathedral for you. You are to be one of God's choristers, and there is to be a continual sacrifice of praise and thanksgiving going up from your heart, with which God shall be continually well-pleased.

And there should be not only the offering of the lips, but the surrender of the life with joy. Yes, with *joy*, and not with *constraint*. Every faculty of our nature should be presented to Him in gladsome service, for the Lord Jehovah is my song as well as my strength.   *W. Hay Aitken*

November 25

Call to remembrance the former days.
Hebrews 10:32

The former days—times of trial, conflict, discouragement, temptation. Did we oftener call these to remembrance, with how much more delight would we make the covert of God's faithfulness our refuge, exclaiming with the psalmist, "Because Thou hast been my help, therefore in the shadow of Thy wings will I rejoice."   *R. Fuller*

November 26

The Lord... thy habitation.   Psalm 91:9

We go home without arrangement. We plan our visits, and then go home because they are over. Duty, want, a host of things lead us forth elsewhere, but the heart takes us home. Blessed, most blessed is he whose thoughts pass up to God, not because they are driven like a fisherman's craft swept by the fierceness of the storm, not because they are forced by want or fear, not because they are led by the hand of duty, but because God is in his habitation and his home. Loosed from other things, the thoughts go home for rest.

In God the blessed man finds the love that welcomes. There is the sunny place. There care is loosed and toil forgotten. There is the joyous freedom, the happy calm, the rest, the renewing of our strength—at home with God.
Mark Guy Pearse

November 27

These have turned the world upside down.
Acts 17:6.

None of these things move me.   Acts 20:24

The men that move the world are the ones who do not let the world move them.   *Selected*

November 28

He touched the hollow of Jacob's thigh in the sinew that shrank.   Genesis 32:32

Whatever it is that enables a soul whom God designs to bless to stand against Him, God will touch. It may be the pride of wealth, or of influence, or of affection, but it will not be spared—God will touch it. It may be something as *natural* as a sinew; but if it robs a man of spiritual blessing God will touch it. It may be as *small* a thing as a sinew; but its influence in making a man strong in his resistance of blessing will be enough to condemn it—and God will touch it. And beneath that touch it will shrink and shrivel, and you will limp to the end of life.

Remember that the sinew never shrinks save beneath the touch of the angel hand—the touch of tender love.   *F. B. Meyer*

November 29

With God all things are possible.   Mark 10:27

Unbelief says, "How can such and such things be?" It is full of "hows"; but faith has one great answer to the ten thousand "hows," and that answer is—GOD!   *C. H. Mackintosh*

November 30

Ye are the temple of the living God; as God hath said, "I will dwell in them and walk in them."   2 Corinthians 6:16

These temples were reared for Him. Let Him fill them so completely that, like the Oriental temple of glass in the ancient legend, the temple shall not be seen, but only the glorious sunlight, which not only shines into it but through it, and the transparent walls are all unseen.
A. B. Simpson

December

December 1

Without Christ. Ephesians 2:12

Without a hope to cheer, a Pilot to steer, a Friend to counsel, grace to sustain, heaven to welcome us, and God to console!   *Selected*

December 2

When I am weak, then am I strong.
2 Corinthians 12:10

This is God's way. We advance by going backward, we become strong by becoming weak, we become wise by being fools.   *F. Whitfield*

December 3

Holy men of God spoke as they were moved by the Holy Ghost.   2 Peter 1:21

The Bible is the writing of the living God. Each letter was penned with an almighty finger. Each word in it dropped from the everlasting lips. Each sentence was dictated by the Holy Spirit. Albeit that Moses was employed to write his histories with his fiery pen, God guided that pen. It may be that David touched his harp and let sweet psalms of melody drop from his fingers, but God moved his hands over the living strings of his golden harp. Solomon sang canticles of love and gave forth words of consummate wisdom, but God directed his lips and made the preacher eloquent. If I follow the thundering Nahum, when his horses plow the waters; or

Habakkuk, when he sees the tents of Cushan in affliction; if I read Malachi, when the earth is burning like an oven; if I turn to the smooth page of John, who tells of love; or the rugged chapters of Peter, who speaks of fire devouring God's enemies; if I turn aside to Jude, who launches forth anathemas upon the foes of God—everywhere I find God speaking. It is God's voice, not man's; the words are God's words: the words of the Eternal, the Invisible, the Almighty, the Jehovah of ages. This Bible is God's Bible; and when I see it, I seem to hear a voice springing up from it, saying, "I am the Book of God. Man, read me. I am God's writing. Study my page, for I was penned by God. Love me, for He is my Author, and you will see Him visible and manifest everywhere."   *Spurgeon*

December 4

They all forsook Him and fled.   Mark 14:50

Separation never comes from His side.
J. Hudson Taylor

December 5

Belshazzar the king made a great feast.
Daniel 5:1

There was one Guest not invited, but He came, and the work of His finger glowed upon the wall.   *Selected*

December 6

He that watereth shall be watered also himself.
Proverbs 11:25

The effective life and the receptive life are one. No sweep of arm that does some work for God but harvests also some more of the truth of God, and sweeps it into the treasury of life.
Phillips Brooks

December 7

And they came unto Him, bringing one sick of the palsy.   Mark 2:3

Had it not been for the palsy, this man might never have seen Christ!   *Selected*

December 8

Bless the Lord, O my soul, and forget not all His benefits...who crowneth thee with loving kindness and tender mercies.   Psalm 103:2,4

We talk about the telescope of faith, but I think we want even more the microscope of watchful and grateful love. Apply this to the little bits of our daily lives, in the light of the Spirit, and how wonderfully they come out!
Frances Ridley Havergal

December 9

When thou passest through the waters I will be with thee.   Isaiah 43:2

God's presence in the trial is much better than exemption from the trial. The sympathy of His heart with us is sweeter far than the power of His hand for us.   *Selected*

December 10

Then shall ye discern between the righteous and the wicked.   Malachi 3:18

Said Anne of Austria to Cardinal Richelieu: "God does not pay at the end of every week, but He pays at last!"   *Selected*

December 11

What is your life? It is even a vapor, that appeareth for a little time and then vanisheth away.   James 4:14

Only one life, 'twill soon be past;
Only what's done for Christ will last.
Selected

December 12

He [Jesus]...looked up to heaven.   Mark 6:41

In working for God, first look to heaven. It is a grand plan. Over and over again our Lord Jesus Christ looked to heaven and said, "Father." Let us imitate Him; although standing on the earth, let us have our conversation in heaven. Before you go out, if you would feed the world, if you would be a blessing in the midst of spiritual dearth and famine, lift up your head to heaven. Then your very face will shine, your very garments will smell of myrrh and aloes and cassia out of the ivory palaces where you have been with your God and Savior. There will be stamped upon you the dignity and power of the service of the Most High God.   *McNeil*

December 13

The disciples were called Christians first in Antioch.   Acts 11:26.

This name suggests that the clear impression made by our character, as well as by our words, should be that we belong to Jesus Christ. He should manifestly be the center and the guide, the impulse and the pattern, the strength and reward, of our lives. We are Christians. That should be plain for all folks to see, whether we speak or be silent.

Is it so with you?   *Alexander Maclaren*

December 14

Having therefore these promises.
2 Corinthians 7:1

The forests in summer days are full of birds' nests. They are hidden among the leaves. The little birds know where they are; and when a storm arises, or when night draws on, they fly, each to his own nest. So the promises of God are hidden in the Bible, like nests in the great forest; and thither we should fly in any danger or alarm, hiding there in our soul's nest until the storm be overpast. There are no castles in this world so impregnable as the words of Christ.
J. R. Miller

December 15

Now abideth faith, hope, love, these three; but the greatest of these is love.
1 Corinthians 13:13 ERV

Love is the greatest thing that God can give us, for He Himself is love. It is also the greatest

thing we can give to God, for it will give ourselves, and carry with it all that is ours.
Jeremy Taylor

December 16

He [Thomas]...said, "Except I shall see...I will not believe...." Jesus...said "...Be not faithless, but believing." John 20:25,27

Every doubt in the heart of a Christian is a dishonor done to the Word of God and the sacrifice of Christ. *Selected*

December 17

Lot...pitched his tent toward Sodom.
Genesis 13:12

Soon Lot moved into Sodom, and before long Sodom moved into him. *Theodore Cuyler*

December 18

Cleanse Thou me from secret faults.
Psalm 19:12

The world needs men who are free from *secret* faults. Most men are free from gross, public faults. *Selected*

December 19

A hearer of the word...a doer of the work.
James 1:23,25

Religion may be learned on Sunday, but it is lived in the weekday's work. The torch of religion

may be lit in the church, but it does its burning in the shop and on the street. Religion seeks its life in prayer, but it lives its life in deeds. It is planted in the closet, but it does its growing out in the world. It plumes itself for flight in songs of praise, but its actual flights are in works of love. It resolves and meditates on faithfulness as it reads its Christian lesson in the Book of Truth, but "faithful is that faithful does." It puts its armor on in all the aids and helps of the sanctuary as its dressing-room, but it combats for the right, the noble, and the good in all the activities of practical existence, and its battle-ground is the whole broad field of life.
John Doughty

December 20

Ye know not what shall be on the morrow.
James 4:14

"Tomorrow" is the devil's great ally—the very Goliath in whom he trusts for victory. "Now" is the stripling sent forth against him.... The world will freely agree to be Christians tomorrow if Christ will permit them to be worldly today.   *William Arnot*

December 21

The sea wrought, and was tempestuous.
Jonah 1:11

Sin in the soul is like Jonah in the ship. It turns the smoothest water into a tempestuous sea.   *Selected*

December 22

Be not slothful, but followers of them who through faith and patience inherit the promises. Hebrews 6:12

God makes a promise. Faith believes it. Hope anticipates it. Patience quietly awaits it. *Selected*

December 23

Go and sit down in the lowest room. Luke 14:10

He who is willing to take the lowest place will always find sitting room; there is no great crush for the worst places. There is no jostling at the back as there is at the front; so if we would be comfortable, we shall do well to keep behind. *Thomas Champness*

December 24

Continue in prayer. Colossians 4:2

Our prayers often resemble the mischievous tricks of children, who knock at their neighbors' houses and then run away: We often knock at heaven's door and then run off into the spirit of the world. Instead of waiting for entrance and answer, we act as if we were afraid of having our prayers answered. *Williams*

December 25

A multitude of the heavenly host praising God, and saying, "Glory to God in the highest." Luke 2:13,14

Angels had been present on many august occasions, and they had joined in many a solemn chorus to the praise of their Almighty Creator. They were present at the creation: "The morning stars sang together, and all the sons of God shouted for joy." They had seen many a planet fashioned between the palms of Jehovah, and wheeled by His eternal hands through the infinitude of space. They had sung solemn songs over many a world which the Great One had created. We doubt not, they had often chanted, "Blessing and honor, and glory, and majesty, and power, and dominion, and might be unto Him that sitteth on the throne," manifesting Himself in the work of creation. I doubt not that their songs had gathered force through ages. As when first created, their first breath was song, so when they saw God create new worlds, then their song received another note; they rose a little higher in the gamut of adoration. But this time, when they saw God stoop from His throne and become a babe hanging upon a woman's breast, they lifted their notes higher still; and reaching to the uttermost stretch of angelic music, they gained the highest notes of the divine scale of praise and they sang, "Glory to God *in the highest*," for higher in goodness they felt God could not go. Thus their highest praise they gave to Him in the highest act of His Godhead.   *Spurgeon*

December 26

God forbid that I should glory save in the cross of our Lord Jesus Christ.   Galatians 6:14

The cross is the great center of God's moral universe! To this center God ever pointed, and the eye of faith ever looked forward, until the Savior came. And now we must ever turn to that cross as the center of all our blessing, and the basis of all our worship, both on earth and in heaven—in time and throughout all eternity.

December 27

He ever liveth.   Hebrews 7:25

It is our hope for ourselves, and for His truth, and for mankind. Men come and go. Leaders, teachers and thinkers speak and work for a season, and then fall silent and impotent. Yet He abides. They die, but He lives. They are lights kindled, and therefore sooner or later quenched, but He is the true Light from which they draw all their brightness, and He shines for evermore. *Alexander Maclaren*

December 28

The friendship of the world is enmity with God.   James 4:4

It is like the ivy with the oak. The ivy may give the oak a grand, beautiful appearance, but all the while it is feeding on its vitals. Are we compromising with the enemies of God? Are we being embraced by the world by its honors, its pleasures, its applause? This may add to us in the world's estimation, but our strength becomes lost.   *Denham Smith*

December 29

She [Hannah]...prayed unto the Lord, and wept sore...she spoke in her heart.
1 Samuel 1:10,13

For real business at the mercy-seat give me a homemade prayer, a prayer that comes out of the depths of my heart, not because I invented it but because God the Holy Ghost put it there, and gave it such living force that I could not help letting it out. Though your words are broken and your sentences disconnected, if your desires are earnest, if they are like coals of juniper, burning with a vehement flame, God will not mind how they find expression. If you have no words, perhaps you will pray better without them than with them. There are prayers that break the backs of words; they are too heavy for any human language to carry. *Spurgeon*

December 30

Noah found grace in the eyes of the Lord.
Genesis 6:8.

Noah found grace in the same way that Paul obtained mercy (1 Timothy 1:16), namely, by mercy's taking hold of him. *Selected*

December 31

Which hope we have as an anchor to the soul.
Hebrews 6:19

Anchor to the throne of God, and then shorten the rope! *Selected*